Our American Century

★

Decade of Triumph · The 40s

★

By the Editors of Time-Life Books, Alexandria, Virginia

With a Foreword by John Robert Slaughter

Contents

★

Foreword

On June 6, 1944—D-Day in France—I was 19 years old and scared to death. I was a sergeant in the 116th Infantry Regiment, the same outfit as Edward Regan, shown at right in that famous photograph by Robert Capa. I came into Omaha Beach about 10 minutes earlier than Ed, maybe 800 yards to the west. At first I froze on the landing-craft ramp because it was bobbing up and down so violently in the surf. It was like riding a bucking bronco. I finally jumped and let the tide carry me in.

On the beach, cross fire from German machine guns was eating men alive. I took off running as fast as I could. Only when I reached the sea wall did I discover that my assault jacket was full of holes.

I hadn't even realized I was being fired on. I got up the cliffs and through the day okay. (So did Ed). My D Company lost about 40 percent of its men—40 killed, 32 wounded. Some of these were boys I had grown up with and played ball with back home in Roanoke, Virginia. And D-Day was just the beginning. For weeks we didn't get a decent meal or a change of clothing and hardly any sleep. I remember days when there were two dead GIs in every foxhole and the ground was all plowed up from shells, and grown men were crying. I was wounded twice but made it across France and Germany with my outfit to meet up with the Red Army at the end of the war.

After I went home in 1945, I was pretty wild. I didn't feel comfortable with anyone unless he had seen combat. Then I buckled down, married, and started a family.

That whole decade was shot through with the war, even though most of us tried hard to forget it. And for a long time, I did forget about the war. Then it all started coming back to me, and I wanted to remember. And when I did, I was proud—proud of myself and my whole generation, for what we had done.

John Robert Slaughter

Lieutenant Walter Chewning scrambles toward the cockpit of an F6F Hellcat that has just crash-landed on the flight deck of the USS Enterprise in early November 1943. Miraculously, the pilot, Ensign Byron Johnson, escaped with only minor injuries.

An eerie light suffuses the shattered jungle of Bougainville as a U.S. tank and infantrymen press the attack. This largest of the Solomon Islands saw intense fighting—often hand to hand—for more than two weeks in March 1944.

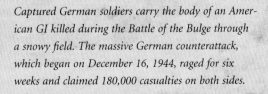

Captured German soldiers carry the body of an American GI killed during the Battle of the Bulge through a snowy field. The massive German counterattack, which began on December 16, 1944, raged for six weeks and claimed 180,000 casualties on both sides.

*A lone figure maneuvers through horrific debris on the Frie-
drichstrasse, one of Berlin's main boulevards, on May 2, 1945—
only hours after the cease-fire that ended the war in Europe.
Heavy Russian shelling and Allied air strikes devastated the
German capital in the war's last days.*

Destiny
in Their Hands

★

ALLIED AND AXIS LEADERS

The numbers were staggering: well over 50 million troops under arms all around the globe, and literally hundreds of millions of lives affected one way or another. But in a very real sense, World War II was a struggle among a mere handful of men—the leaders of the principal nations in conflict. Their decisions drove the great armies, but their own personal strengths and weaknesses had as much to do with the final outcome as their strategizing. They were the war's protagonists, and how the plot would unfold ultimately depended on them.

For Franklin Delano Roosevelt, the role was a natural. He had made a career of overcoming obstacles, fighting back from a crippling bout with polio in 1921 and going on as president to help lead the nation out of the Depression. And here now, as the 1940s dawned, were new challenges: first, to prepare a reluctant nation for its inevitable entry into war; and second, to win that war. He would succeed in this as he had so often before, blending swift, effective action with inspiring words that gave voice to America's unique blend of confidence, courage, and goodwill.

What appealed to people most was how plainly he spoke—just as if he were a friend telling you something. To sell the concept of lend-lease, a program to keep Britain supplied with war matériel, he used a simple analogy: "Suppose my neighbor's home catches on fire, and I have a length of garden hose. . . ." America was won over.

His resolve as steadfast as his gaze, President Franklin Delano Roosevelt delivers a fireside chat to the nation on the eve of D-Day, June 5, 1944.

Champion of the Realm

At their first official meeting off Argentia, Newfoundland, in August 1941, it was instant friendship. Both FDR and Winston Churchill came from privileged families, both had been naval leaders during World War I, and both now served as heads of state. Each had flair, and each was capable of a stirring oratory that in the worst of times brought out the best in his people. And like FDR, Churchill saw earlier than many in his country the danger posed by Adolf Hitler—an awareness that made him a political pariah in the 1930s. "[Prime Minister] Chamberlain has a lust for peace," Churchill scoffed in 1937. It took Germany's invasion of Norway early in 1940 for the truth to hit home. Within months, Churchill became prime minister. He was just the sort of tonic the British people needed—a leader with nerves of steel and the gift of speech to brace them for the bombs that would soon be peppering London.

During the war, more than 1,700 letters would pass between Churchill and Roosevelt. "The Former Naval Person," Churchill signed himself, relishing their bonhomie. But there were characteristic differences, too, and they surfaced as early as the conference at Argentia. The prime minister, always more point-blank in dealing with adversaries, wanted to issue a firm Anglo-American declaration against Japanese encroachment in the southwest Pacific; FDR preferred the diplomacy of delay, giving the Japanese a month or two to cool their heels. It took Pearl Harbor to finally settle the matter.

The consummation of what was known as the Anglo-American common-law alliance came when Churchill made his historic address to a joint session of Congress in 1941. Aware of anti-British sentiment in the Senate, the prime minister had spent days fretting about his speech. He strode up to the podium and hooked his thumbs under his lapels. "I cannot help reflecting," he began, "that if my father had been American and my mother British . . . I might have got here on my own." At the end, the audience jumped to their feet in thunderous applause. Churchill, relishing the moment, flashed a "V" for victory, and the marriage was sealed.

The picture of confidence, Winston Churchill relaxes in an air-raid shelter during an RAF-Luftwaffe air battle over Dover in September 1940.

I cannot forecast to you the action of Russia. It is a riddle wrapped in a mystery inside an enigma.
—1939

Victory at all costs, victory in spite of all terror, victory however long and hard the road may be; for without victory there is no survival.
—1940

We shall fight them on the beaches, we shall fight them on the landing grounds, we shall fight them in the fields and in the streets, we shall fight in the hills; we shall never surrender.
—1940

Let us therefore brace ourselves to our duties and so bear ourselves that if the British Empire and its Commonwealth last for a thousand years men will still say, "This was their finest hour."
—1940

Here is the answer which I will give to . . . Roosevelt. . . . Give us the tools and we will finish the job.
—1941

Hitler is a monster. . . . Not content with having all Europe under his heel . . . this bloodthirsty guttersnipe must launch his mechanized armies upon new fields of slaughter, pillage and devastation.
—1941

Never give in. Never give in. Never, never, never, never, never—in nothing great or small, large or petty—never give in except to convictions of honour and good sense.
—1941

I felt as if I had been struck a physical blow. My relations with this shining personality [Roosevelt] had played such a large part in the long, terrible years we had worked together. Now they had come to an end.
—on the death of Roosevelt, 1945

It has been said that democracy is the worst form of Government except all those other forms that have been tried from time to time.
—1947

The Terrible Simplifier

Like Roosevelt, Adolf Hitler loved to talk. But while FDR inspired Americans by dressing lofty democratic ideals in homespun words, the Führer fed the anger of his own people by spewing out nationalist diatribes. The speeches he gave were an incoherent jumble of folk sentiment, racist slurs, and xenophobia that held Germans in thrall. Reduced by the "death sentence of Versailles" to humiliation and economic despair, they were a nation in search of scapegoats. Adolf Hitler, the terrible simplifier, took it upon himself to deliver.

During World War I he had won the Iron Cross for bravery, then—embittered over Germany's defeat—joined other disgruntled nationalists to form the Nazi Party. Jailed after an abortive attempt to overthrow Bavaria's republican government in 1923, he wrote *Mein Kampf*, the dense Nazi tome that blamed the war on Jews and Marxists. It wasn't until the severe depression of 1929 that his movement caught on; four years later, President Paul von Hindenburg named him chancellor of Germany. With swift efficiency and the aid of his Nazi cronies—including Göring, Himmler, and Goebbels—the new chancellor seized control of every facet of the German state, enacting anti-Semitic laws and setting up concentration camps to liquidate his enemies.

Before the close of the decade, he would be waging war on virtually all of Europe. "I do not ask my generals to understand my orders," Hitler remarked, "but only to carry them out." This micromanaging of strategy would turn out to be a fatal error. Spare, socially ill at ease, a Spartan who neither smoked nor drank, the Führer grew increasingly isolated until in 1941, deaf to all warnings, he made two reckless decisions: to wage a two-front war, and to disperse his eastern force across the vast spaces of Russia.

Another fatal mistake would be his miscalculation of American resolve. Incredibly, Hitler's view of American soldiers was derived from the film *The Grapes of Wrath*. The U.S. population was "an uprooted mob" of "miserable and degenerate farmers," he concluded, who would never beat the solid sons of dictatorship. Germany's military mastermind reduced a complex world to simple formulas. It would be his undoing.

Hitler rails against the enemies of Germany in a prewar speech. His gestures were carefully rehearsed for maximum dramatic effect.

From *Mein Kampf*:

The world would then see, as quick as lightning, to what extent this Reich, people, party, and these armed forces are fanatically inspired with one spirit, one will.

A majority can never replace the man. . . . Just as a hundred fools do not make one wise man, a heroic decision is not likely to come from a hundred cowards.

All propaganda has to . . . adapt its spiritual level to the perception of the least intelligent of those towards whom it intends to direct itself.

I go the way that Providence dictates with the assurance of a sleepwalker.
—1936

I shall stand or fall in this struggle. I shall shrink from nothing and shall destroy everyone who is opposed to me.
—1939

A world-wide distance separates Roosevelt's ideas and my ideas. Roosevelt comes from a rich family and belongs to the class whose path is smoothed in the democracies. I was the lonely child of a small, poor family and had to fight my way by work and industry.
—1941

After fifteen years of work I have achieved, as a common German soldier and merely with my fanatical will power, the unity of the German nation, and have freed it from the death sentence of Versailles.
—1941

This war . . . is one of those elemental conflicts which usher in a new millennium and which shake the world once in a thousand years.
—1942

Is Paris burning?
—1944

Caesar the Second

It has been said that Benito Mussolini's single legacy to Italy was getting its trains to run on time. In fact, for almost two decades after 1922—the year he marched on Rome with his Fascist Party—this flamboyant son of a blacksmith toiled to uplift his nation. Racked by debt, poverty, and unemployment, Italy was in desperate need of a leader. *Il Duce* threw himself into the job. Tirelessly traveling around the countryside to promote public works and agricultural self-help projects, he would strip to the waist and spend hours wielding ax and shovel, brawny muscles glistening in view of a reverent public.

Accolades poured in from all over Europe. Hitler modeled his fledgling Third Reich on Fascist Italy, adopting everything from its nationalized industry to its rigid salute—everything, that is, but its leader's flamboyant personal style. The drab Teuton could never compete with a man who fancied himself Caesar the Second, showing up at their first encounter in Venice wearing spurred boots, a fringed fez, and a blaze of medals across his chest.

In 1936 the tide would turn. With the might of the Third Reich swelling, Mussolini began to imitate Hitler. He passed anti-Semitic decrees, invaded Ethiopia and Albania, and then in 1940 announced that Italy was joining the Axis. His ministers were aghast: The nation wasn't equipped for a massive military undertaking. Indeed, as Herr Hitler spent the next years blitzing through Europe, Caesar would end up watching from the sidelines.

The Italian proletariat needs a bloodbath for its force to be renewed. —1920

Italy! Italy! Entirely and universally Fascist! The Italy of the blackshirt revolution, rise to your feet; let the cry of your determination rise to the skies. —1933

We have buried the putrid corpse of liberty. —1934

A gaudy plume topping his immaculate uniform, Mussolini leads a military parade. Style often outranked substance in the Italian dictator's calculations.

The Powerless God

On December 6, 1941, President Roosevelt sent Japan's emperor, Hirohito, a message: Consider withdrawing Japanese forces from Indochina. Fate was moving more swiftly, of course, but it is unlikely that the shy monarch with a passion for marine biology—his area of expertise was jellyfish—could have acted on the request in any event. A clique of jingoists virtually ruled Japan. In need of a figurehead who would inspire their troops to valor, they had restored the emperor's traditional quasi-divine status and encouraged his veneration. The Son of Heaven was the ideal pawn: untouchable, blinding to behold—and perfectly impotent.

From the beginning the emperor had had handlers. Born in 1901 and whisked from his parents' arms 10 weeks later, he spent his childhood under the guidance of a string of tutors, who drummed imperial duties into his head. At the age of 20, in a glimmer of independence, he became the first emperor to set foot outside Japan when he made a tour of Europe that inspired a lifelong taste for Western suits, sports, and breakfasts of toast and eggs. In most respects, however, the traditions built during 26 centuries of dynasty kept him cowed.

At a meeting in 1941, as Japan's ministers pressed for an attack on Pearl Harbor, the soft-spoken monarch quoted a poem by his grandfather: "Why do the winds and waves of strife disrupt peace?" He was ignored. Not until August 1945, when Hiroshima and Nagasaki lay in atomic ruins, would Hirohito openly defy the military leaders by announcing Japan's surrender. The next year brought another shocking announcement: This notion about the emperor's divinity, Hirohito proclaimed, is simply false.

[The army] is using silk floss to suffocate me. —1936

I cannot bear to see my innocent people suffer any longer. Ending the war is the only way to restore world peace and to relieve the nation from the terrible distress with which it is burdened. —1945

Revered even after his nation's defeat, Hirohito and the empress Nagako ride through the Imperial Plaza in Tokyo in November 1946.

"Nothing Human to Get Hold Of"

During a toast at the Tehran conference in 1943—a meeting of the Allies' Big Three—the Soviet Union's leader, Joseph Stalin, announced that 50,000 Germans should be rounded up after the war and shot. Britain, Churchill retorted, would never stand for such butchery. With tempers about to flare, Roosevelt broke in: only 49,000, he quipped, offering a mock compromise.

Roosevelt spent most of the war trying to woo Stalin with breezy goodwill. His effort was largely wasted; the deeply suspicious Marshal, who felt his Western allies were in league against him, proved to be fiercely single-minded in pursuing his agenda. Roosevelt ultimately despaired of reaching him on a personal level, commenting that in Stalin he could find "nothing human to get hold of."

The son of a shoemaker and an illiterate peasant, Stalin had passed the years leading up to the Bolshevik Revolution in the Marxist underground, slipping from jail more than once and staging bank robberies to fill the movement's meager coffers. The revolution resulted in his appointment as secretary-general of the Communist Party in 1922. After consolidating his power, he set about implementing his vision for the country. In a series of Five-Year Plans starting in 1928, agricultural collectivization and industrialization were pushed through with dehumanizing, breakneck speed.

Responding to murmurs of discontent, Stalin launched the Great Purge and through labyrinthine maneuvering snuffed out every trace of opposition in the party, in the army, and among the citizenry. A decade after the First-Year Plan was begun, the Soviet Union showed astonishing industrial progress—vehicle manufacturing, for example, had risen a whopping 15,000 percent—but it came with a hefty price. Seven million people had fallen victim to Stalin, including his own in-laws. Distraught over her husband's brutality, his wife killed herself. When his son Yakov tried to do the same and botched the attempt, Stalin's reaction was sardonic: "Ha! He can't even shoot straight."

The fate of Poland having been decided in his favor, Soviet premier Joseph Stalin looks smug while posing for photographers at the Potsdam conference in 1945.

To choose one's victim, to prepare one's plan minutely, to slake an implacable vengeance, and to go to bed—there is nothing sweeter in the world.
—1923

The state is an instrument in the hands of the ruling class, used to break the resistance of the adversaries of that class.
—1924

A single death is a tragedy, a million deaths a statistic.
—attributed to Stalin

The Pope! How many divisions has he got?
—as quoted by Churchill

History shows that there are no invincible armies, and never have been.
—1941

It may be asked, How could the Soviet Government have consented to conclude a nonaggression pact with [Germany]? . . . I think that not a single peace-loving state could decline a peace treaty with a neighboring state even though the latter was headed by such fiends and cannibals as Hitler and Ribbentrop.
—1941

To the enemy must not be left a single engine, a single railway car, not a single pound of grain or a gallon of fuel.
—1941

This war is unlike all past wars. Whoever occupies a territory imposes his own social system. Everyone imposes his system as far as his army can advance.
—1945

America Goes to War

★

They were the pride of America: young men at their physical peak, fresh faced but purposeful, innocent but somehow ready for the task at hand. And as America became the last great nation to join the second global conflict of the century, they confidently shouldered the burdens their country was placing on them. In the course of the fighting they would be alternately exhausted and energized; they would feel fear and show courage; they would make—and lose—lifelong friendships with their buddies in arms; they would be wounded and maimed; and they would die. After it all, the vast majority of them would come home victorious and in one piece, but changed forever.

What gave them the edge that led to triumph? Of all the factors to consider, near the top of the list must come the American spirit itself, so movingly apparent in the faces of the boys who went to war *(left)*. Marjorie Haselton of Massachusetts may have put it best, in a letter she wrote to her husband on the very last day of the war: "You and I were brought up to think cynically of patriotism by the bitter, realistic writers of the twenties and thirties. This war has taught me—I love my country and I'm not ashamed to admit it anymore. I am proud of the men of my generation. . . . None of you fellows wanted the deal life handed you—but just about everyone of you gritted your teeth and hung on. You boys proved that you had a fighting spirit and team work that couldn't be beaten."

Unaware of the brutal fighting they were soon to face in the weeks to come, U.S. soldiers prepare to go ashore during Operation Torch, the invasion of North Africa, in November 1942.

1940

★

The Gathering Storm

On New Year's Day 1940, most Americans were happily going about their normal business. They were lining up at movie theaters to see the film version of Margaret Mitchell's novel *Gone With the Wind.* They were debating whether Tennessee or Southern California would take the Rose Bowl. They were feeding nickels into roadhouse jukeboxes to hear Wee Bonnie Baker warble "Oh, Johnny! Oh!" And they were speculating on whether President Franklin Delano Roosevelt would throw his hat in the ring and run for an unprecedented third term.

If Americans thought at all about the war under way overseas, they likely considered the fighting someone else's problem. True, Germany had clamped an iron fist around Central Europe, and Japan was advancing on China. But the troubles were two broad oceans away. Besides, four months had passed since Adolf Hitler had sent his panzers into Poland in September 1939—and by so doing embroiled himself in war with Britain and France. The conflict was at a seeming standstill, and Americans held fast to the pledge of neutrality made by their government in the 1930s. A poll conducted in December 1939 showed that fully two-thirds of the public were opposed to taking sides in the war.

Angry Czechs crowd the streets of Prague as German troops enter the city on March 15, 1939. When Hitler went on to take Poland six months later, Britain and France declared war, but America still clung to neutrality.

But some in the nation were watching the situation closely. The press was devoting more and more space to reports on the events abroad. And when Roosevelt gave his State of the Union address in January, he asked Congress for $1.8 billion to finance the greatest peacetime military buildup in the history of the United States.

Most Americans reacted to Roosevelt's foresight with skepticism or outrage. But as spring came around, the situation in Europe suddenly worsened. In two months Hitler's troops overran Denmark, Norway, Belgium, Luxembourg, and the Netherlands. Next the Nazis crushed France, whose modernized army had been considered the best in the world. Then Italy, seeking a share in the spoils, entered the war on the side of Germany. "The hand that held the dagger," FDR intoned, "has struck it into the back of its neighbor." The two strong fascist nations, calling themselves the Axis powers, ruthlessly set about seizing the rest of Europe.

As they did so, Americans faced a hard new reality. Hitler now controlled all of western Europe. Only Britain and the ocean stood between Germany and the United States—the Atlantic did not look quite so broad now. The effect of all this on American opinion was a complete about-face: By May 1940, two-thirds of the public favored giving aid to Britain. Pledging that the U.S. would "extend to the opponents of force the material resources of this nation," President Roosevelt asked Congress for another $4.8 billion to further beef up American armaments. He urged manufacturers to bring the production of planes up to 50,000 a year—a quota they soon topped by producing an average of 60,000 planes annually.

In 1940 moviegoers flocked to see Gone With the Wind, a tale of one woman's will to survive amid the devastation of the Civil War. The first Hollywood blockbuster shot in color, it offered welcome distraction from the disturbing war news from Europe.

Taking a poke at Adolf Hitler, Charlie Chaplin played the role of tyrant Adenoid Hynkel in the 1940 comedy The Great Dictator. The movie received mixed reviews at home but was a hit in war-ravaged Britain.

Isolationist Backlash. Despite the turn in opinion, much of the nation still believed the U.S. should take no sides. Some 700 citizens' committees sprang up to debate the wisdom of what seemed to be a drift toward war. In less than six months, the America First Committee gathered 60,000 members—among them Alice Longworth, daughter of former president Teddy Roosevelt, and Colonel Charles A. Lindbergh, the Lone Eagle of 1927, who had been well entertained in Berlin by Field Marshal Göring following his historic transatlantic flight. "The three most important groups which have been pressing this country toward war are the British, the Jewish, and the Roosevelt Administration," said Lindbergh during a speech in Des Moines, Iowa.

A high-school student who heard those words later recalled, "All I could think was: It's not the British, the Jewish, or the Roosevelt administration that's firing torpedoes at American ships. It's the Nazis." Nevertheless, the isolationists branded FDR a warmonger, and in the summer of 1940 their worst fears were confirmed. At that time the U.S. Army ranked 17th among the world's armies in total manpower and modern weapons, a fact that galled many patriots. In June, Senator Edward R. Burke and Representative James W. Wadsworth brought before Congress the Selective Training and Service Bill, which called for the first peacetime draft in the nation's history.

Isolationists were nearly apoplectic. "If you pass this bill," thundered Senator Burton K. Wheeler of Montana, "you accord Hitler his greatest and cheapest victory to date." But the majority of the nation stood squarely behind the draft bill, and the feeling in Congress was equally strong: It became law on September 16.

Willkie Tries to Win. Those who saw in the draft the demise of democratic practices took heart in the upcoming presidential elections. FDR delighted his admirers by becoming the first incumbent ever to run for a third term. "We Want Roosevelt!" roared the delegates when his name was placed in nomination that July at the Democratic National Convention in Chicago.

"Let us stop this hysterical chatter of invasion."

Charles A. Lindbergh

Charles Lindbergh addresses a rally in New York City sponsored by the America First Committee, whose aim—articulated on the patch at top—was to preserve American neutrality. Lindbergh resigned his commission in the Air Corps Reserves that year but after Pearl Harbor flew 50 combat missions as a civilian.

In Philadelphia, meanwhile, the Republicans nominated dark horse Wendell Willkie, a one-time Democrat who was president of a large utilities firm. His rumpled suits and habit of wearing the same tie day after day gave him the air of a country bumpkin, but the self-deprecation concealed a powerful and cosmopolitan mind. Willkie was the most formidable opponent Roosevelt had faced in some 30 years of political life. Ideologically, there was little difference between the candidates. On the domestic front, Willkie agreed with Roosevelt's program of social reform, and on foreign policy, both candidates favored aid to Britain. Faced with no substantive issue upon which to base their challenge, Republicans tried to create one out of Roosevelt's bid for a third term. But the voters didn't take the bait. When November came, more than 22 million Americans voted for Willkie—the largest total racked up by any Republican in the century. But 27 million others voted to keep Roosevelt in office.

With his victory at the polls certain, the president set about securing further aid for Britain, which was now in desperate straits. Since August 8, 1940, Germany had been raining bombs on British cities. CBS correspondent Edward R. Murrow began broadcasting live from London every evening, and his sonorous opening, "This . . . is London," was soon familiar to Americans. Familiar, too, both as background on

Murrow's radio broadcasts and on newsreel soundtracks, were the wail of air-raid sirens, the scream of German bombs, and the thunder of antiaircraft fire.

By late fall, it was unclear how much longer Britain could hold out. Apart from the human toll imposed by war, the country's coffers were nearly empty. In just over a year of fighting, the government had spent $4.5 billion for armaments in the U.S. alone; now it had less than $2 billion left in reserve. But Roosevelt had a plan. He called a news conference on December 17 and after saying, "I don't think there is any particular news, except possibly one thing," went on to discourse for 45 minutes on a concept that was big news indeed.

The president introduced what came to be known as the Lend-Lease Act, which provided for aid to "any country whose defense the President deems vital to the defense of the United States." The benefi-

Wendell Willkie arrives in Elwood, Indiana, to accept the Republican presidential nomination. Campaign buttons for both sides focused on FDR's run for a third term (opposite). Headlines blared the election's final result (below).

The New York Times.

ROOSEVELT ELECTED PRESIDENT; CERTAIN OF 429 ELECTORAL VOTES; DEMOCRATS KEEP HOUSE CONTROL

The dome of St. Paul's Cathedral in London stands out among the smoke and flames of an intense fire-bombing raid on December 29, 1940. Although the bombs caused 1,500 blazes in the East End alone, volunteers inside the church saved the famous landmark from serious damage.

ciaries of lend-lease would not have to pay in cash for the aid; instead they would reciprocate with other goods and services. In addition, the bill gave FDR the power to name any item he chose a defense article and designate any country he chose to receive it.

General Hugh Johnson, once head of Roosevelt's National Recovery Administration but lately a defector from the administration's ranks, roared that the Lend-Lease Act was "humanitarian lollipopping all over the world." Representative Hamilton Fish of New York cried that the bill would leave Congress "with no more authority than the German Reichstag." But most Americans supported the measure, and the bill became law on March 11, 1941.

Prime Minister Winston Churchill hailed the news, and his fellow Britons joyously flew American flags on the streets of London. The Italian press made the saber-rattling observation that "Roosevelt's gesture may cause many unpleasant surprises to England and the United States in the Pacific." Hitler said defiantly that lend-lease or no, "England will fall."

A Significant Step. Within a few months, the significance of lend-lease became apparent. Whereas the United States had managed to put together only 16 tanks in March 1941, by the end of the year 951 tanks had been shipped to Britain. Food shipments reached one million tons, while the overall output of trucks, planes, guns, and ammunition was stepped up at a comparable pace. This effort, while filling the pressing needs of Britain, simultaneously stocked America's own arsenal.

As many an America Firster had feared, lend-lease turned out to be a prelude to much deeper American involvement in the war—but not in the way anyone had expected. The growing military power of the U.S. and the strengthening of its bond with Britain loomed as a threat not just to Germany but also to Japan, which would soon take action in response. And the lightning bolt that would strike American reluctance finally dead would come from the East, at a place known affectionately to locals as Pearl.

The radio dispatches of CBS correspondent Edward R. Murrow, shown here on a London street, helped bring home to Americans the plight of the British people. Many of his on-the-spot reports were delivered against a backdrop of air-raid sirens and exploding bombs.

1941

★

Into the Fray

At about 1:40 p.m. on Sunday, December 7, 1941, the terse telegram reached the White House: "AIR RAID PEARL HARBOR—THIS IS NO DRILL." A Japanese strike force consisting of six aircraft carriers and a powerful support force had begun unleashing its lethal covey of 353 planes. To gain air superiority, they struck first at airfields where U.S. planes were closely parked wing to wing. Then they swooped down to send torpedoes smashing into Battleship Row.

Stunned navy crewmen fought back heroically. Aboard the stricken battleship *West Virginia,* a black mess attendant, Doris Miller, raced topside to help drag his mortally wounded skipper to cover and then grabbed a machine gun and shot down four enemy planes. But the attack was so overpowering that in two hours the U.S. had suffered grievous losses. More than 2,400 servicemen were killed. No fewer than 347 airplanes were destroyed or disabled. Eight battleships, three destroyers, and three cruisers were sunk or severely damaged.

"Great ships were dying before my eyes! . . . At first I didn't realize that men were dying too."

Mrs. John B. Earle, whose home overlooked Battleship Row

A fiery explosion rocks the destroyer Shaw after fire from a direct hit touched off the forward magazine. Remarkably, the ship was later repaired and survived to sail again.

On Ford Island, in the middle of Pearl Harbor, American sailors work among the ruins of the naval air station while to the east clouds of smoke billow from the burning battleship Arizona.

Pearl Harbor—a bay on the southern coast of Oahu, Hawaii's largest island—was the home base for the U.S. Pacific Fleet. The possibility of a sneak attack on Pearl long had been a standard part of strategic thinking for military planners in both the United States and Japan. How to achieve it had even been the final examination question posed to every graduating class at the Japanese naval academy since 1931. Moreover, as early as January 1940, the U.S. ambassador to Japan had warned of talk that a surprise attack might be mounted against Pearl Harbor.

But Roosevelt and Churchill had only briefly considered the problem of their potential joint enemy in the Pacific; they counted on avoiding a showdown with Japan in order to buy time to defeat Hitler. Nevertheless, in July, after the Japanese had occupied rubber-rich French Indochina, Roosevelt retaliated by freezing Japan's assets in the U.S. and cutting off trade in strategic goods. The embargo deprived Japan of about 80 percent of the oil it needed and stepped up pressure on the civilian government. In October, the moderate premier resigned and was succeeded by General Hideki Tojo, a hawk who had the ear of Emperor Hirohito. Tojo, accelerating preparations for war, gave his envoys in Washington a deadline—the end of November—to win a lifting of the oil embargo.

Because the U.S. had cracked the top-secret Japanese code known as Purple, Roosevelt was able to follow much of the intrigue in Tokyo. But with his eye still on Europe, he nonetheless hoped to keep the Japanese at the negotiating table. An early war in the Pacific, he said, would mean "the wrong war in the wrong ocean at the wrong time." Wishing didn't make it so, however, and when the attack came, it caught the U.S. woefully unprepared.

The Japanese bombs were still falling when the news reached most Americans via radio. Some were certain at first that it was just another hoax perpetrated by Orson Welles, who had panicked listeners three years previously with his highly convincing broadcast of a fictitious invasion from the planet Mars. In recent public opinion polls, eight out of 10 Americans had favored staying out of the war. But

"We could hear tapping all over the ship, SOS taps, no voices, just eerie taps from all over. There was nothing we could do for most of them."

Seaman Joseph Hydruska, 22, member of rescue party, describing the scene on the battleship *Oklahoma*, which had taken six torpedoes below the water line and was about to capsize

The View From Up There

This long-lost photograph shows the view from a Japanese plane during the first minutes of the surprise attack on Pearl Harbor. The picture was discovered in Japan after the war. The attack, launched from six carriers sailing 220 miles to the north, began at 7:57 a.m. Here, several of the battleships in the foreground already have been struck by torpedoes. Smoke rises in the distance from bombs dropped on Hickam Field.

A phonograph record preserves parts of Roosevelt's speech to Congress on December 8; the flip side features an address by Winston Churchill. "We are all in the same boat now," FDR told Churchill.

"Yesterday, December 7, 1941—a date which will live in infamy—the United States of America was suddenly and deliberately attacked by naval and air forces of the empire of Japan."

President Roosevelt, December 8, 1941

now they reacted with shock, anger, and resolve. "Everything changed," a young playwright named Arthur Miller realized. "Immediately, finally, the whole country had a purpose."

The Call to Arms. On the day after Pearl Harbor, President Roosevelt—his polio-ravaged legs held straight by 10-pound steel braces—stood before a joint session of Congress. He asked "that the Congress declare that since the unprovoked and dastardly attack by Japan . . . a state of war has existed." Within hours, both houses approved the declaration of war with one dissenting vote. In the House of Representatives, so isolationist only four months earlier that it had passed the extension of the draft by a single vote, only Congresswoman Jeannette Rankin of Montana, a pacifist, dissented—as she had in 1917, when she voted against United States entry into World War I.

Even as Roosevelt spoke, the war was spreading. The attack on Pearl Harbor was aimed at crippling the U.S. Pacific Fleet to protect the Japanese eastern flank during incursions into Southeast Asia. Now Japanese bombers on December 8 hit the island outposts of Guam and Wake and then smashed U.S. air power in the Philippines in preparation for a full-scale invasion two weeks later. By the end of the year, Japanese troops occupied Hong Kong and had invaded Thailand and Malaya. U.S. Marine defenders on Wake repulsed one landing attempt and, before they were overwhelmed, radioed the brazen request that would become a leatherneck legend: "Send us more Japs!"

On the home front, far from bombs and bullets, jittery civilians prepared for the air raids and invasion many felt certain would come. In Washington State, farmers on Whidbey Island patrolled Puget Sound every night. In Los Angeles, sirens shrieked false air-raid alerts. Practice blackouts got off to a spotty start in Seattle, where hundreds of citizens smashed the windows of stores that failed to turn out their lights.

Speaking to a joint session of Congress on the day after Pearl Harbor, Roosevelt asks for a declaration of war against Japan. An audience of 60 million Americans—an unprecedented number—listened by radio.

Preparing for the worst in San Francisco, workmen construct a barrier of sandbags to protect windows of the Pacific Telephone and Telegraph Building. After Pearl Harbor, citizens across the country hurried to get ready for bombing raids that never came.

The recruiting poster above was one of many colorful works of art commissioned by the army, navy, and marines to entice young men to enlist.

"Well, that's it—I'm going to enlist tomorrow."

Harold Ludeker of Milan, Indiana, after hearing about the attack on Pearl Harbor

At Fort Dix, New Jersey, an army draftee whose sole remaining claim to dignity is his hat gets a smallpox inoculation in one arm and a typhoid injection in the other.

Shipping Out

When war was declared, so many young men rushed to join up that some military recruiting stations remained open around the clock. In the first week after Pearl Harbor, the army, navy, and marines signed up nearly 25,000 recruits. Many volunteers sought to avoid the infantry by choosing special branches of service. In Detroit, three generations of the same family—grandfather, father, and son—showed up to enlist in the navy. A high-school student in suburban Philadelphia, trying to sharpen his vision so he could be an Army Air Corps fighter pilot, ate so many carrots his skin briefly turned a bright orange.

Thousands entered service after receiving greetings from their local draft board. On December 22, Roosevelt signed an expansion of selective service that required the induction of men aged 20 to 44 and the registration of all males 18 to 65. All four of Roosevelt's sons—James, Elliott, Franklin Jr., and John—were already officers in the armed forces, and on his 60th birthday the president himself received his own draft card.

Recruits were swallowed up by an alien world of inch-long doctor's needles and half-inch crewcuts, uniforms that seldom fit and shoes that constantly had to be spit-shined. They endured reveille, night marches,

Through an aisle of comrades idly waiting their turn, sailors shouldering heavy duffel bags prepare to ship out from the big naval base in San Diego.

screaming sergeants, and the degrading duty known as KP, for "kitchen police." They learned a new lingo in which the most important word was SNAFU, for "Situation Normal—All Fouled Up." They wore World War I–vintage helmets and practiced combat with cardboard artillery and trucks hung with placards proclaiming them to be tanks.

The Longest Good-Bye. The marriage rate soared after Pearl Harbor. An estimated 1,000 women a day were marrying servicemen. A few months earlier, the motivation for many marriages had been to help the man avoid the draft. Now young couples sought an emotional anchor among the uncertainties of war. Some wives attempted to stay near their husbands, taking lodging close to the training camps. But all too soon came the day when the man had to ship out overseas, and the good-byes were said on docks and in bus and train stations all over the country.

Wives and parents then could do little more than wait and worry and follow the news, trying to imagine what their loved ones were going through. Every family eagerly watched the mail for letters, which offered at least a momentary reassurance. And everyone dreaded the arrival of one of those telegrams that began, "We regret to inform you . . ."

The warm love of a last embrace, the inconsolable tears of a child, the empty grief of loneliness: Emotions ran close to the surface as loved ones bid farewell to their departing sweethearts, fathers, and husbands.

The Sign of Victory

In a 1941 radio broadcast, Belgian refugee Victor de Lavaleye suggested that patriots scrawling "R.A.F." on buildings (the abbreviation for Britain's Royal Air Force) should instead use the letter *V*—the first letter in *victory* in almost every European language. The United States joined the new campaign with gusto, its citizens doing everything from wearing victory pins to tapping *V* in Morse code on drinking glasses. This *dot dot dot dash* began every BBC news brief, often followed by the famous *da da da dum* opening of Beethoven's Fifth—*V* in Roman numerals—Symphony.

Winston Churchill popularized the two-fingered "V for victory" salute, making it the symbol of the Allies' unshakable resolve. Soon everyone from schoolchildren to Hollywood stars was copying the gesture.

Tote bag

Inspirational buttons

REMEMBER
PEARL
HARBOR

COMMITTEE TO DEFEND AMERICA

for
VICTORY

BROOCH

...V...

JOIN THE MILLIONS FOR
VICTORY
A NEMO PRODUCT

V   V

FOR VICTORY

V-shaped pins and brooches

THIS IS A
V
HOME

Poster for window display

AXIS   AXIS   AXIS

V

Playing cards with dictators' faces

Drinking glass

VICTORY CHICKEN
from
Dee-Jay Farms
RURAL ROUTE NO. 1
LOVELAND, OHIO

VICTORY
CHICKEN
from
Dee-Jay Farms
RURAL ROUTE NO. 1
LOVELAND, OHIO

Food carton

DECONTAMINATION CORPS

A lean, young Joe DiMaggio waits on deck at Yankee Stadium in 1941. His pursuit that year of the longest consecutive hitting streak in major-league history captured the attention of fans and non-fans alike throughout the nation.

Arts and Entertainment

One of the most influential films ever made, Citizen Kane (above) was written and directed by Orson Welles, who also starred as Charles Foster Kane, the newspaper tycoon modeled on publishing mogul William Randolph Hearst.

The patriotic hit "Boogie Woogie Bugle Boy" was sung by the Andrews Sisters (below) in the movie Buck Privates. The film starred Abbott and Costello, who posed with the sisters for the cover of the song's sheet music (right).

I'm tickled to death it's all over," said Yankee slugger Joe DiMaggio (left) upon ending baseball's record-setting hitting streak of 56 consecutive games. Less than a year later, fans would bemoan the loss of Joltin' Joe to the air force, where he served until the war was over.

Searching high and low for civilian heroes, *Time* named Disney's baby elephant, Dumbo (above), Mammal of the Year, calling him "the face of a true man of good will among all the grim and forbidding visages of A.D. 1941." At the movies, Citizen Kane (above, right) opened to critical raves, proving that a ruthless antihero also could ignite America's imagination.

Shouldering makeshift litters to carry their sick and disabled comrades, exhausted American and Filipino captives approach the prison enclosure at Camp O'Donnell—the final destination for the 65-mile-long Bataan Death March. Of the 76,000 troops who surrendered, only 54,000 made it to the camp, where they continued to die at a rate of up to 400 a day.

1942
★
Setbacks and Successes

January 1942 brought more bad news from the Pacific: Manila, the capital of the Philippines—a United States possession since the turn of the century—had fallen to the Japanese. The defenders—both U.S. and Philippine troops—withdrew to the nearby Bataan Peninsula, and Far East commander General Douglas MacArthur moved his headquarters into a tunnel fortress on Corregidor, a small island located two miles off the tip of the peninsula. They were in desperate straits, and they were also on their own: Even before the fall of Manila, Roosevelt and his top generals had already resigned themselves to the loss of the Philippines.

What followed was three months of hell for the troops in the Bataan jungle, who were starving, sick with tropical diseases, and under constant attack. Without reinforcements, they had little chance of beating back the Japanese, although they did manage some temporary successes. Finally, on April 9, they gave up the fight. For them, hell was about to get worse.

General Douglas MacArthur (inset, left), sporting his gold-braided Filipino field marshal's cap, confers with Philippine president Manuel Quezon on the island of Corregidor.

Soldiers surrender Corregidor, the sole remaining Allied garrison in the Philippines, on May 6, 1942. "I shall always see a vision of grim, gaunt, ghastly men, still unafraid," said MacArthur.

At a relocation center in Arizona, the Hirano family proudly display a photograph of their soldier son. All-Japanese regiments became some of the most decorated American combat teams in the war.

The Japanese now poured a concentrated bombardment on Corregidor so intense that it altered the island's contours. On May 5 came the last radio message from the command tunnel: "The jig is up. Everyone is bawling like a baby." The next day Corregidor was surrendered, along with the rest of the Philippines.

Meanwhile, the Bataan captives had begun a forced march up the peninsula to a prison camp 65 miles away. It would be known as one of the most brutal episodes of the entire war. Stragglers were clubbed, stabbed, or shot; in one two-hour killing frenzy some 350 Filipino soldiers were bayoneted and beheaded. The final tally was appalling: more than 20,000 dead.

Defeated but uncowed, MacArthur—who had left Corregidor in March under FDR's express orders—vowed to return and free his beloved Philippines. It would be an inspiring pledge.

Mistrust at Home. Even before the Philippines fell, American frustration at its initial helplessness against Japan found troubling expression back home. On February 19, President Roosevelt signed an executive order permitting the forced evacuation of 120,000 people of Japanese ancestry, 77,000 of whom were U.S. citizens. Most were given just days to dispose of their homes, businesses, and possessions, and then were taken under military guard by train to internment camps.

Many of the camps were in remote desert locations. "Sand filled our mouths and nostrils and stung our faces and hands like a thousand darting needles," recalled one internee. Entire families lived in one small room equipped only with cots and a pot-bellied stove.

To the surprise of camp residents, in 1943 the army announced it would accept Japanese American recruits. Some volunteered out of patriotism, others simply to leave the camps. The all-Japanese units served with distinction—a source of pride to many of their dispossessed relatives, who would have to wait until war's end to put their lives back together.

"Herd 'em up, pack 'em off, and give 'em the inside room in the badlands."

Hearst newspaper column

In plain sight of a guard tower, three Japanese American boys gaze beyond the barbed-wire enclosure of their wartime home. "We would play near barbed wire," recalled one young internee. "There was a target range not far from us. I can remember hunting around for bullet shells." To make life seem as normal as possible, children attended school, joined Scout troops, and played baseball.

Passing Muster at "Fort Lipstick"

May 27, 1942, the opening day of registration for the Women's Army Auxiliary Corps (WAAC), caught recruiters off guard: More than 13,000 volunteers signed up, eager to contribute to the war effort—and to prove their mettle. Their first chance came at Fort Des Moines, Iowa, the WAAC training center, better known to media wags as Fort Lipstick: While an enlisted man stood sheepishly by with smelling salts lest anyone faint, unfazed rookies lined up for their inoculations and took them with barely a flinch.

In little more than a year, the "Petticoat Army" proved so capable that it became an integral part of the service, renamed the Women's Army Corps. By war's end more than 300,000 women would join Uncle Sam in U.S. Marine, Navy, and Coast Guard support units as well, working every job from cook and typist to truckdriver and airplane mechanic. Although forbidden to fire a gun in combat, clearly Eve could keep up with Adam—a wartime lesson that would not be lost in the decades to come.

WAAC director Oveta Culp Hobby inspects a rookie unit (above). "Wackies," as a jeering press dubbed them, stoically endured a regimen that included trench digging and survival-in-the-field exercises.

"They're a damn sight better than we ever expected they would be. I honestly didn't believe they could do it."

Colonel Don C. Faith,
Commander, Fort Des Moines

A pilot training for the Women's Auxiliary Ferrying Squadron solos her plane over Texas (right). The ferry pilots' primary mission was flying new planes from factories to their assigned air bases. Recruiting posters like the ones below inspired thousands of women to serve their country in uniform.

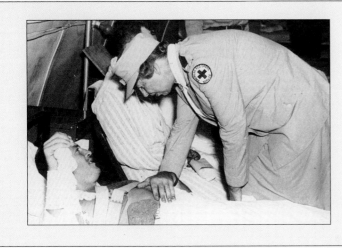

An American Mom in the Pacific

A tireless crusader for women in the military, Eleanor Roosevelt still had energy left over for fighting men. The first lady made a marathon tour of hospitals and Red Cross clubs in the Pacific, "followed," said one witness, "by a brace of generals and admirals teetering on the edge of collapse." Her sincere effort to speak with every wounded man she met inspired lingering gratitude. As one soldier recalled, "She was something . . . none of us had seen in over a year, an American mother."

Doolittle's Daring Tokyo Raid

This force is bound for Tokyo!" Aboard the air-craft carrier USS *Hornet*, that cry was answered with reverberating cheers by the crew about to launch the first air raid on Japan.

The plan was simple but ambitious: Land-based army B-25s, refitted to make them lighter and increase their range, would be launched from a carrier positioned far enough outside Japan's 500-mile defense perimeter to be reasonably safe from attack. Carrier-based navy planes had too short a range for the job, and since the December 1941 bombing of Philippine airfields, no American land-based planes lay in range of the Japanese home islands.

Heading the mission was Lieutenant Colonel James H. Doolittle, a World War I pilot who drilled the five-man crews in getting the modified bombers aloft after extremely short takeoff runs. The raid was scheduled for April 19. Early on the 18th the *Hornet* was spotted by a Japanese patrol boat. The carrier was still 150 miles from the planned launch point, but it was now or never. Extra fuel was put aboard each of the 16 planes, and with Doolittle taking the lead, the B-25s swarmed toward Tokyo and three other target cities.

The bombers came in at treetop level to evade radar—"low enough," Doolittle later recounted, "to see the expressions on the faces of the people. It was one, I should say, of intense surprise." The planes then climbed to 1,500 feet, dropped their bombs, and headed for an airfield deep inside China's borders.

Only two planes reached unoccupied China. Two others crash-landed in Japanese territory. One bomber low on fuel landed in the Soviet Union; the crews of 11 others, unable to locate the landing field through the heavy cloud cover, bailed out.

Although the damage inflicted on Japanese soil was negligible, the psychological effect was enormous: The enemy that had once considered itself invincible had lost face. American civilians and soldiers who had agonized through the dark months of Pacific defeats found their spirits—and their resolve—renewed.

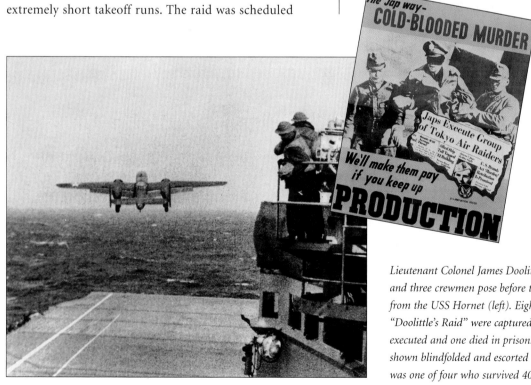

Lieutenant Colonel James Doolittle (opposite, second from left) and three crewmen pose before their B-25 prior to takeoff from the USS Hornet (left). Eight out of the 80 participants in "Doolittle's Raid" were captured by the Japanese; three were executed and one died in prison. Lieutenant Robert Hite, shown blindfolded and escorted by soldiers in the poster above, was one of four who survived 40 months in prison camp.

Workers at Boeing's no. 2 Seattle plant pose in front of the 5,000th Flying Fortress to come off their assembly line. Virtually everyone who worked on the plane signed it somewhere, and in a last loving sendoff they pushed it out onto the tarmac by hand.

Prodigious Output

July 1, 1940 to July 31, 1945

Aircraft	296,429
Naval ships	71,062
Cargo ships	5,425
Artillery	372,431
Small arms	20,086,061
Rounds of ammunition	41,585,000,000
Aircraft bombs (tons)	5,822,000
Tanks, self-propelled guns	102,351
Trucks	2,455,964

Winning the Production War

America's arms buildup was a marriage of government oversight and private enterprise that yanked the country out of depression, making its economy the most productive on earth. Traditionally, U.S. capitalists were suspicious of government direction. To woo them, Washington handed out rich rewards for defense contracts; and to encourage plants to meet weapons quotas, it awarded the coveted Army-Navy E (for "excellent") pennant, shown at top. The results are reflected in whopping statistics: By 1944, U.S. industry was churning out a B-24 every hour, a jeep every two minutes, and 50 percent more armaments overall than the Axis powers. For workers,

the payoff was sometimes deeply personal. One story that inspired more than a few involved a seaman named Elgin Staples, whose life belt had saved him from drowning when his ship went down off Gaudalcanal. Later, he discovered a stamp on the belt indicating it had come from his hometown of Akron, Ohio—and had been inspected and packed by his own mother.

The new submarine Peto (inset), decked in bunting, broadsides the water at its official launch from a Wisconsin shipyard in 1942.

The Bandanna Brigade

With so many men overseas, America's wartime industry relied heavily on women to keep up its frenetic pace. Between 1940 and 1944 the number of employed women rose from 12 million to 18.2 million, many lured into factories by rousing propaganda like Westinghouse's "We Can Do It!" poster (above). Other ads reflected some ambivalence about females in the workplace. "A woman is a substitute, like plastic instead of metal," one government brochure said bluntly. Fueling reservations were media vignettes of neglected children and absenteeism on the part of working mothers, problems that Eleanor Roosevelt, who was quick to recognize women's genuine job skills, tackled in her campaign for government-sponsored day care.

Despite the criticisms, the cold, hard cash women earned was certainly nothing to sniff at, and most relished the role of wage earner. "We now have about $780 in the bank and 5 bonds," Polly Crow, who worked for a company making landing craft, wrote to her husband. "As soon as I get the buggie in good shape I can really pile it away."

With acetylene torches (left), women bevel armor plating for tanks at a Gary, Indiana, steelworks. Poster girl Rosie the Riveter (below, left), complete with trademark bandanna, was based on an actual woman, Rose Monroe (below), who worked in an aircraft plant in Ypsilanti, Michigan.

The Tide Begins to Turn

Had Americans not been forewarned, the battle plan of Admiral Isoroku Yamamoto, the mastermind behind Japanese naval strategy in the Pacific, might well have succeeded. Undaunted by a clash in the Coral Sea off Australia's northeast coast in early May, where the American fleet had narrowly thwarted Japan's southward expansion, Yamamoto began methodically shifting battleship, carrier, and cruiser positions. Naval intelligence informed Admiral Chester Nimitz, commander in chief of the Pacific Fleet, that Yamamoto had big plans, but it didn't know where he'd strike next.

By mid-May the cryptanalyst who had decoded Japanese intercepts and predicted the operation in the Coral Sea announced the enemy's apparent new target: Midway. About 1,150 miles northwest of Hawaii, Midway Island could serve the Japanese as a steppingstone to Alaska and ultimately the U.S. mainland. In reality, Yamamoto's main objective was to draw the U.S. fleet into a fight and smash it. But as Yamamoto's armada closed in on Midway and his bombers took to the air on June 4, they were met by a smaller but equally determined U.S. force. Over the next few hours, dive bombers and torpedo planes dropped their deadly cargo while fighters and shipboard guns shot them down, with the Americans suffering heavy losses. But in one well-timed attack, U.S. dive bombers struck three carriers, including the *Akagi*, whose planes had just finished refueling and were all destroyed in the ensuing conflagration.

By dawn on June 5, a stunned Admiral Yamamoto retreated westward. "The Midway occupation is canceled," he radioed to his forces, adding in a whisper, "The price is too high." The price was high indeed. The defeat at Midway blunted the Imperial Navy's striking power, decisively shifting the balance of might in the Pacific.

Guadalcanal. American forces may have shown that they could best the Japanese on the sea, but they had yet to prove themselves on land. That test came two months later, when U.S. intelligence learned that enemy soldiers were building an airstrip on Guadalcanal.

Under a sky smoky from antiaircraft fire, flames burst from the carrier Yorktown during the battle for Midway. Two torpedo hits punched holes in the port side, prompting the captain to hoist the blue-and-white signal to abandon ship.

Located in the Solomons, a thousand miles east of Australia, the island was a strategic spot for two reasons: It lay in the shipping lane regularly used by the U.S. to ferry men and matériel for the Pacific offensive; and enemy fliers taking off from Guadalcanal would be able to attack Australia and those islands still held by the Allies.

The U.S. sent 11,000 marines in to take the island. Wading ashore on August 7, they met with little resistance, securing the beachhead and the unfinished airstrip in a day. Offshore, however, trouble was brewing. The Allied fleet accompanying the invasion soon found itself under a surprise night attack that in less than 40 minutes decimated its ranks. The marines were now virtually on their own.

Time and again the Japanese launched attacks on the marine perimeter around the airstrip, but they never broke through. The runway was completed early on, and soon U.S. planes were helping support the ground action. When the first dive bombers arrived, "I was close to tears," said General Alexander Vandegrift, the marine commander. But the fighting had scarcely begun. The Japanese kept landing more troops, and sea battles raged offshore. The breakthrough finally came toward the end of the year, when Admiral William Halsey arrived with his fleet and army reinforcements. In one last bloody battle, the exhausted marines—many sick with malaria, dysentery, and jungle rot, and all longing to leave the tropical hell behind—dealt a punishing blow to the ene-

"What I'd give for a piece of blueberry pie."

A U.S. Marine on Guadalcanal, 1942

Marines slog through water on the main street of their headquarters in the middle of a coconut grove on Guadalcanal. Standing water from tropical downpours bred the malaria-carrying mosquitoes that plagued American and Japanese troops alike.

Immediately following the attack on Pearl Harbor, the Sullivan brothers—from left, Joseph, Francis, Albert, Madison, and George—enlisted in the navy. After their deaths at Guadalcanal when the cruiser they all served on was destroyed, their lone sibling, Genevieve, enlisted in the Waves.

my, who withdrew to more northerly islands. It was the first ground loss for the Japanese since the beginning of the war.

Five Precious Boys. The U.S. Navy fought seven major battles for Guadalcanal, including a particularly bitter encounter in mid-November. Among the crewmen on the *Juneau* were five brothers, the Sullivans from Waterloo, Iowa *(left)*. The brothers—ranging in age from Albert, 20, to George, 28—had insisted on staying together.

On the morning of November 13 torpedoes intended for another target struck the *Juneau* with shattering force. "She blew up with all the fury of an erupting volcano," recalled an officer. "A minute or so later, we could see nothing of this fine 6,000-ton cruiser or the 700 men she carried." George was the only Sullivan brother to survive the carnage. Tying together rafts and life nets, the hundred or so oil-soaked survivors drifted under the broiling sun with little food or water, waiting for rescue. Over the course of 10 days at sea, the men succumbed one by one to their wounds, to exposure, or to shark attacks, until only 10 were left. George Sullivan died on the fifth night. News of the deaths was not made public until January, when it became clear that none of the brothers had survived. Thenceforth, the navy prohibited family members from serving on the same vessel.

Their mother, Alleta Sullivan, somehow weathered the tragedy. "The boys always wrote at the end of their letters, 'Keep your chin up.' And now's a good time to do just that."

A Torch for North Africa

T his is the largest landing operation that has ever taken place in the history of the world," marveled Adolf Hitler upon learning in early November 1942 that more than 800 Allied ships were approaching North Africa. It was a massive bid to end the desert war, which had been raging since December 1940, when the British forced the occupying Italian army to retreat to Libya and Hitler sent aid in the form of Lieutenant General Erwin Rommel and the newly formed Afrika Korps.

Involving the cooperation of multiple Allied forces, the landing in French Morocco and Algeria, code-named Operation Torch, was staggering in its sheer magnitude. Well over 100,000 American and British soldiers hit the beaches from ships laden with 11,000 tons of food, 10 million gallons of gasoline, and 500,000 pairs of shoes. The landing itself was far from smooth: Vehicles fell overboard, troops waded ashore on the wrong beaches, and huge waves swamped and overturned landing craft. But after a few bloody skirmishes, opposition from the Vichy French—German collaborators who held France's North Africa territories—collapsed. Real challenges awaited to the east.

A few days before the Torch landings, British lieutenant general Bernard Montgomery (top, left) finally brought the Desert Fox, Erwin Rommel (top, right), to bay at El Alamein—a turning point in the desert war.

Carrying an American flag to identify themselves to possibly sympathetic French forces in the area, U.S. infantrymen come ashore near the Algerian port of Oran on November 8, 1942. Loyal more to expediency than to anything else, the Vichy French—puppet rulers of occupied France and North Africa—soon capitulated and joined the Allies.

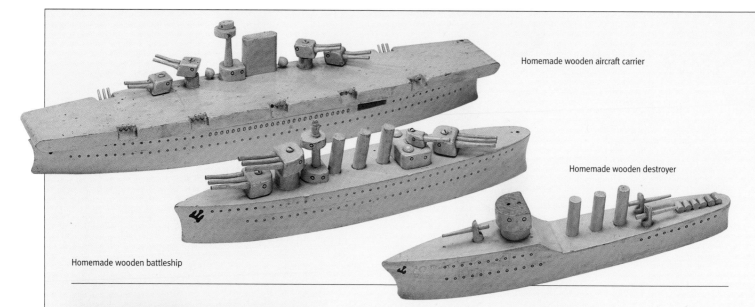

Homemade wooden aircraft carrier

Homemade wooden destroyer

Homemade wooden battleship

Toys Go to War

Her sacrifice as great as anyone's, a toddler offers her rubber dolly to a scrap-collection depot. Deprived of rubber, some toymakers turned to a largely untried new material—plastic.

America's entry into the war generated both an opportunity and a crisis for toymakers. To most children, the war seemed a great adventure with endless possibilities for fun and excitement, but just as the demand for war toys began to grow, the government passed a series of Limitation and Conservation Orders prohibiting the use of traditional toy materials such as steel, tin, rubber, and lead. Since prewar inventories could still be marketed, some companies sold off their existing stock before converting their factories to war production. Other manufacturers chose to remain in the business and began producing lines of toys featuring creative use of nonstrategic materials such as wood and cardboard. Home workshops played their part as well *(top);* many children treasured these one-of-a-kind gems, made just for them—and destined to become family heirlooms.

Wind-up tank

Hollow-cast lead parachutist and infantrymen

Wartime coloring books

Patriotic "Poison This Rat"
pinball game

Balsa-and-plastic
toy truck

"Little Army Nurse" play set

Board game with glow-
in-the-dark counters

Arts and Entertainment

THE SAD SACK

O ne of the war years' great films, *Casablanca (above and left),* opened on Thanksgiving Day to wild acclaim. The romantic melodrama of espionage and love sundered by war was set in Morocco, where two weeks earlier the Allied forces had landed. With some of cinema's most memorable phrases, including "Here's looking at you, kid," and "We'll always have Paris," the movie won the Oscar for best picture.

George Baker's satirical cartoon "The Sad Sack" *(right, top)* kept America laughing, but the year's sentimental tug came from Irving Berlin's "White Christmas" *(right, middle),* sung by Bing Crosby in the film *Holiday Inn;* its simple nostalgia hit home with everyone who was missing a loved one.

A frustrated sergeant shows the perpetually inept Sad Sack (above) how to use a bayonet in the popular cartoon about GI life.

The hit song "White Christmas" (right) expressed a sentimental longing for a family holiday at home. In contrast, Edward Hopper's starkly realistic painting Nighthawks (below) pictured the solitude of city life.

Star-crossed lovers Rick and Ilsa (left), played by Humphrey Bogart and Ingrid Bergman, lock eyes one last time in the final scene of Casablanca.

1943

★

War on All Fronts

The Allies' January 1943 conference was a top-secret event. From Washington on a train ostensibly bound for Hyde Park, Roosevelt was rerouted to Miami and flown to Casablanca, which was crawling with Axis spies. Leaving nothing to chance, the Americans deployed antiaircraft batteries around the villa headquarters and called in medical officers to test every morsel of food before Roosevelt and Churchill sat down to eat. The press knew nothing of the 10-day conference until it was over.

All the intrigue delighted Roosevelt, who needed a break from the strains of wartime Washington. Still, hard strategic decisions had to be hashed out by the president, the prime minister, and their combined chiefs of staff. With Stalin absent (he was preoccupied with the fighting at Stalingrad), most of the decisions fell Churchill's way—among them, a joint bombing campaign against Germany, the delay of a cross-Channel assault until 1944, and most immediately, the invasion of Sicily.

That invasion was part of Churchill's pet strategy to pierce Europe's "soft underbelly." But first North Africa had to be cleared of Axis forces, and already the Allied

On a side trip to Marrakesh during their Casablanca conference in January 1943, Roosevelt admires the sunset as Churchill looks pensively on (inset). Lovers of nature both, the two Allied leaders relished such shared moments.

Stars designating their respective ranks, Generals Teddy Roosevelt (far left), Terry Allen (center), and George Patton observe action in Tunisia. "Old Blood and Guts" Patton's fiery oratory helped harden green troops for battle: "We won't just shoot the sonsabitches—we're going to cut out their living guts and use them to grease the treads of our tanks."

The British First Army came from the west, Montgomery's Eighth Army from El Alamein in the east, to corner Axis forces in Tunisia's tip. Two months later, an Allied armada would launch Operation Husky—the invasion of Sicily. Axis troops escaped across the Straits of Messina into Italy, where they kept the Allies fighting until April 1945.

Defending Kasserine Pass, American troops fire 105-mm howitzer shells at German positions on February 20, 1943. Although after eight days the Americans would prevail, the quick capitulation of more than 2,000 U.S. troops was an international embarrassment. "The big-mouthed Yankees," Goebbels scoffed, hadn't even met select troops. British general Harold Alexander called the Americans "mentally and physically soft."

"Gentlemen, tomorrow we attack. If we are not victorious, let no man come back alive."

General George Patton on the eve of the attack on El Guettar, March 16, 1943

campaign there had met with delay. Three days after the Operation Torch landings, Lieutenant General Dwight D. Eisenhower sent the British First Army with American elements racing toward Tunisia in the western half of a pincers movement; the other half was British general Bernard Montgomery's Eighth Army, at that time chasing Rommel from the east across the plains of Libya. Eisenhower expected quick results. Within weeks, however, winter rain turned Tunisian soil into a gooey quicksand that trapped tanks and sucked the boots off men's feet.

Another setback occurred at Kasserine Pass. By February, Major General Lloyd Fredendall's Second Corps, the U.S. sector of the Allied front, was scattered across Tunisia's Eastern Dorsal Mountains, and when early on Valentine's Day Rommel's 10th Panzer Division surged through Faïd Pass, U.S. troops retreated in panic to defensive positions in the Western Dorsals. One of the passes there, the Kasserine, was a narrow gateway to the Allied base at Tébessa. American defensive fire took up position in the basin beyond Kasserine, and on February 19 managed to halt the panzers as they emerged from its bottleneck. Hours later, however, phantom infantrymen began dropping from Kasserine's northern ridges. Unnerved by their sudden appearance out of nowhere, a company of American engineers bolted and set off another wave of panic.

Although Allied reinforcements would eventually turn back the blitz, Fredendall was sacked. In came Major General George S. Patton, charging to the front to whip the cowed troops into shape. Over the coming months a revitalized Second Corps would redeem its reputation, in March repelling a fierce assault in the El Guettar valley by Rommel's 10th Panzer Division, and on May 7, in northern Tunisia, capturing Bizerte.

Six days later Axis troops now at bay in northeastern Tunisia surrendered. The citizens of Tunis were jubilant. Even the vanquished showed some relief: Most Germans, having endured many grueling months of desert warfare, willingly filed into their prison compounds.

The Blue and the Gold

In a tradition dating back to World War I, families who had sent a son off to war hung a special banner in their window: a flag with a blue star in the middle. By 1943 there were so many boys under arms that these blue-star banners—some with two, three, four, or more stars for as many sons—were almost as common a sight on Main Street as the Stars and Stripes itself. But as the fighting intensified in North Africa and, for the first time, the casualties started to mount up (right), more and more of those blue stars were  *exchanged for gold ones, betokening the death of a son. And the noblest citizens back home became the Gold Star Mothers, who met and formed clubs. In many ways, these women represented America's resolve in the face of terrible sacrifice. "There'll be plenty more dead," warned one Gold Star Mother. "I hope we catch those dirty rats."*

Citizens of Monreale, in Sicily, cheer as their American attackers-cum-liberators roll by on the way to Palermo. Everywhere they went, the American troops —many of Italian stock—were welcomed by joyful civilians, who exchanged food and wine for cigarettes and candy, the GI's international currency.

On to Sicily. Thus was the springboard secured for Operation Husky—the invasion of Sicily. On July 10 and 11, soldiers from Patton's Seventh and Montgomery's Eighth Army poured out of their transports onto the island's beaches in a smooth landing. The air component fared less well. Among other glitches, U.S. airborne reinforcements flew over Gela at the tail end of a German bombing attack; confused American gunners fired on their own transport planes and shot down 23, killing 410 soldiers.

Aggravating matters, Allied command rivalry boiled over. The battle plan called for Montgomery's army to spearhead the invasion by pressing north along the east coast toward Messina while Patton's army protected his left flank. Chafing at this support role, the hotheaded American sought permission to make a westward probe of the island, captured Palermo, then raced to Messina and beat Monty by a hair.

"Where have you tourists been?"

U.S. soldier to a column of British tanks arriving in Messina

Sicily fell quickly. Italian soldiers who had become pawns to Hitler's monomania surrendered in droves. Now the stage was set in turn for the invasion of mainland Italy. And so on September 9, almost a week after Montgomery landed on Italy's toe, the U.S. Fifth Army streamed onto the narrow plain at Salerno expecting an easy drive north to Naples. Almost immediately, German reinforcements unleashed a savage counterattack. So much for a soft underbelly. In the coming months the Allied drive up Italy's mountainous spine would prove to be a long, painstaking grind.

GIs enter the outskirts of Messina just ahead of the British, wrapping up a successful Operation Husky. There was only one glaring Allied failure: In a textbook evacuation, the Axis departed Messina with more than 100,000 troops, thousands of tons of matériel, and 12 mules.

Sacrificing for Final Victory

When America entered the war in December 1941, its citizens were called upon to make sacrifices that even the generation of the Great Depression could scarcely imagine. Food was strictly rationed, and almost everything that Americans liked to eat—meat, coffee, butter, cheese, sugar—was controlled by a point system that required retailers and consumers to juggle a host of stamps, stickers, and coupons. To supplement their diets, many patriotic civilians became part-time farmers, tending "victory gardens." Even in cities, thousands tilled small plots of vegetables in whatever open space was available *(opposite)*.

Gasoline rationing limited the average driver to only three gallons of gas per week; on top of that, car owners had to display mileage-ration stickers on their windshields. Rubber was in such short supply that worn tires had to be turned in before ration cards could be issued for replacements. To boost supplies of the raw materials needed for defense, America went on the biggest scavenger hunt in its history. Citizens joined in nationwide scrap drives targeted at everything from iron and steel to nylon stockings and cooking grease.

Despite some grumbling, confusion, and a bit of cheating, Americans came through. For many, doing without was their most tangible contribution to the cause.

A patriot surrenders her used stockings at a government collection bin. Reclaimed silk and nylon was used in the production of such martial items as parachutes, glider towropes, and powder bags for artillery.

Ration books, mileage cards, and reminders to plan food purchases became facts of life in wartime America. At left, New Orleans victory gardener Harry Ducote tends part of his downtown parking lot planted with vegetables.

Making Scrap Count

1 tire	=	12 gas masks
1 shovel	=	4 hand grenades
1 lawn mower	=	6 three-inch shells
1 radiator	=	17 .30-caliber rifles

Paying for the War

In addition to the many sacrifices they had to make in food, mobility, and all manner of consumer goods, the American public also had to pay the enormous cost of fighting the war. The total in military expenditures was staggering—more than $330 billion—and no one expected that increased taxes could even come close to covering the full amount. With so little to buy, however, many Americans did have extra money at hand, and the government financiers soon found a good way for them to apply it to the war effort. Beginning in 1941, the Treasury issued interest-bearing War Bonds in denominations ranging from $25 to $10,000. By the war's end ordinary citizens—exhorted by advertising, national personalities, and mass rallies—had bought some $36 billion worth of bonds.

Posters (the one at lower left was by Norman Rockwell) evoking the fear of Nazi domination and the loss of freedom were created to sell War Bonds. Radio star Kate Smith, seen above opening a bond drive in New York, used her hit shows to raise $600 million in bond sales.

A swing band perched atop a giant cash register swaps music with a navy brass band during a 1944 War Bond drive in New York's Times Square. Giant parades and bond rallies helped build a sense that all American citizens were "doing their part."

Yankee Doodle Airmen

They hit the shores of England in mid-1942, the men of the U.S. Eighth Air Force, cocky greenhorns flying planes with names like Hot Lips and Ima Vailable and preaching the gospel of daytime bombing to an RAF that had already given up on it. The muscle behind their argument was a pair of bombers, the B-24 Liberator and the B-17 Flying Fortress. These fast, high-altitude planes had something that British bombers lacked: the Norden bombsight. The Norden, according to reports, was so accurate it could land "a bomb in a pickle barrel," pinpointing enemy targets and limiting civilian casualties. The British were deeply skeptical. Heavy losses from their own daylight bombing early in the war had left them determined to stick with nighttime saturation bombing. With the two allies clinging to separate strategies, a compromise was struck at Casablanca: "bombing the devils around the clock," as Brigadier General Ira Eaker, head of the Eighth Air Force Bomber Command, put it to Churchill.

Six months later the devastating effects of this joint campaign were visited on Hamburg, Germany's largest port. Operation Gomorrah began on July 24, 1943, when 740 RAF bombers entered German air space, released 92 million strips of tinfoil to jam enemy radar, then went swarming past the confused defenses and sent their bombs spinning down. Over the next two days a total of 121 Fortresses attacked Hamburg's shipyards and a power plant. The "thunderbolt saturation" lasted until August 2, with the RAF on the night shift, the Eighth Air Force on the day, dropping 51 tons of bombs a minute at the peak and whipping up a firestorm that uprooted trees like toothpicks, hurled molten chunks of metal through the air, incinerated citizens holed up in bomb shelters, and left a smoking ghost town in its wake.

For the crew of a B-24 Liberator, sheepskin flight suits (top) offered little protection against the chill of subzero temperatures at 25,000 feet and above. The Eighth Air Force would later introduce electric flight suits. Oxygen masks (bottom) chafed the skin but could not be pulled off for more than a few seconds without imperiling the wearer.

" . . . like a clammy hand clutching the lower part of your face."

Description of oxygen mask worn by American aircrews

B-17 Flying Fortresses turn for home after bombing a Focke Wulf aircraft factory at Marienburg, deep in German territory. The October 1943 raid left the 100-acre factory—a major production center for German fighters—in ruins.

"It was like sitting in the boiler of a hot-water heater that was being rolled down a steep hill."

B-24 pilot Charles W. Paine, on being fired at by Luftwaffe fighter planes

Firefighters spray thousands of gallons of foam on a B-24 Liberator after it crash-lands at its base in England. Crash-landings, the result of crippling damage from enemy fire—or simply running out of fuel on the way home—were common.

For the Eighth Air Force, though, Gomorrah was a short-lived success. Little more than two weeks later, 376 Fortresses flew missions against the southeastern German towns of Regensburg, site of a Messerschmitt fighter plant, and Schweinfurt, where engine ball bearings were manufactured; 60 planes failed to return to base and another 47 were so crippled they had to be scrapped. In October, after a second attack on Schweinfurt that resulted in equally dismal losses, Eaker put a stop to Eighth Air Force raids over deep enemy territory.

Schweinfurt highlighted the flaw in American strategy: Without long-range fighter escorts, daylight bombers were open targets for enemy interceptors. Up to this point U.S. fighters had been able to accompany bombers only on the first leg of their long-distance missions. Now the fighters were outfitted with drop tanks that once spent could be jettisoned for extra speed and maneuverability. By December 1943 the Eighth Air Force was ready

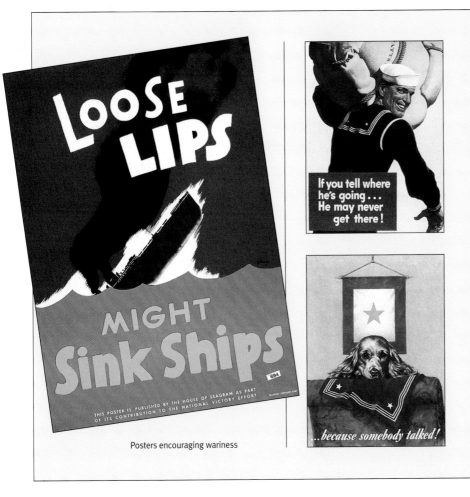

Posters encouraging wariness

Spies Among Us

From the beginning of the war, officialdom had worried about spies—and with good reason. In June 1942 German U-boats dropped off eight saboteurs and crates of explosives on beaches in Long Island and Florida. The enemy agents had all lived in the States before and passed easily for Americans. Their mission: to sabotage U.S. industry. The scheme fell apart in less than two weeks, when two of the men sought out the FBI and made a full confession. In 1944 another Nazi sub landed spies; again they were caught. Such incidents persuaded Americans to take extraordinary precautions. Weather reports were prohibited for two years—so as not to aid possible enemy bombing raids. Radio stations canceled man-on-the-street interviews and musical-request shows for fear that enemy agents might broadcast coded messages through them. And government propagandists ordered up posters like those at left, often tugging at heartstrings to keep everyone on guard.

to send massive bombing missions against distant German targets. Crucial to the success of these raids was the P-51B Mustang, the best all-round fighter of the war. Equipped with auxiliary tanks, it had a range of 850 miles and could escort bombers almost anywhere in Germany.

Through all this the British had come to admire their guests for their innovation—and stamina. U.S. aircrews could remain at altitudes of 26,000 feet without fainting, the London *Evening Standard* marveled, speculating that it was because American boys played baseball. The myth of the American superbody was rooted in the demanding reality of bombing missions. Crews would spend up to 10 hours in cramped, freezing quarters loaded down by 60 pounds of gear and struggling to stay alert during tedious stretches that could suddenly erupt in danger—from Ger-

man fighters roaring out of nowhere, bombers in tight formation colliding, antiaircraft fire, disorienting fog, and "gremlins" like inexplicably clogged fuel lines. Anyone deserved respect who survived—and, of course, many didn't. In the latter half of 1943, prior to the long-range fighter's appearance, roughly a third of U.S. bomber crewmen perished before their quota of 25 or more missions was completed.

"The trouble with the Yanks," the British had complained when their brash comrades first arrived in England, "is they're overpaid, oversexed, and over here." By the end of 1943, with U.S. airmen having proved their mettle and honed their daylight bombing strategy in ways that would turn the tide of the war, that celebrated lament was not so easily bandied about.

A Volunteer Army to Rout GI Blues

One way civilians contributed to the war effort was attending to soldier morale. Concern for homesick draftees prompted many groups—including the YMCA and the Salvation Army—to tackle the problem together by forming the United Service Organizations. USO centers sprang up in every American town near a military base or major transit point, offering movies, dances, hot food, a room to write a letter, even a shoeshine. For troops overseas, the USO sponsored shows from Burma to Belgium starring the Andrews Sisters, Bob Hope, Martha Raye, and another 7,000 entertainers who thought of themselves as "soldiers in grease paint."

Soldiers and sailors packed Broadway's Stage Door Canteen to mingle with celebrity waiters and jitterbug with actresses like Dorothy McGuire (left). While McGuire risked her toes for the cause, Bob Hope traveled on combat tours with the USO. Below, Hope ribs servicemen at a hospital in the South Pacific.

Marlene Dietrich (above), German expatriate and GI favorite, brought USO shows to the front lines.

Singer and film star Lena Horne was especially popular with black GIs. Here she shares the stage with an army band in a postwar engagement.

Hollywood's Heroes in Uniform

When actor Sterling Hayden moved from screen wars to the real thing, he announced, "I don't want to go on imitating men and that's all there is to it." More than a handful of Hollywood stars apparently felt the same way: Indeed, a sixth of the film industry—both actors and actresses—served in uniform. Clark Gable flew bombing missions over Germany. Jimmy Stewart joined him, after making Army Air Force recruiting films asking prospective pilots to "consider the effect these shining wings have on the gals." John Wayne, Hayden, and director John Ford volunteered for secret missions with the Office of Strategic Services (OSS). Ford directed the OSS field photo unit. Wayne was too famous to go undercover, but Hayden smuggled weapons past German blockades to the Yugoslav underground.

Major Jimmy Stewart is decorated for a raid over Germany.

Four weeks before the war's end, Private Mickey Rooney hams it up for infantrymen in Kist, Germany. Metro-Goldwyn-Mayer waged its own war to keep the baby-faced star making movies, but the draft board finally got its man, and the army tasked him with entertaining front-line troops.

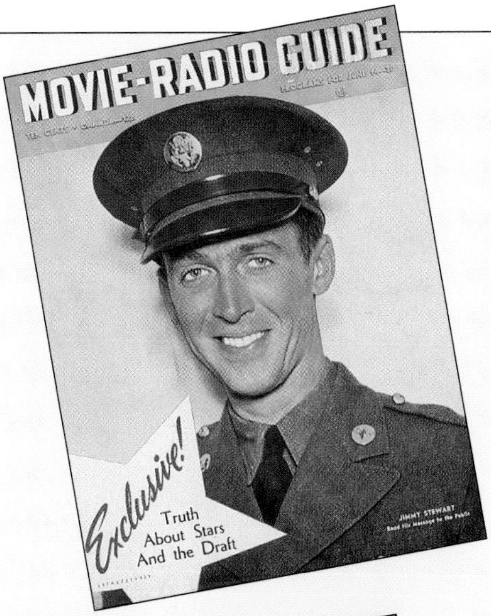

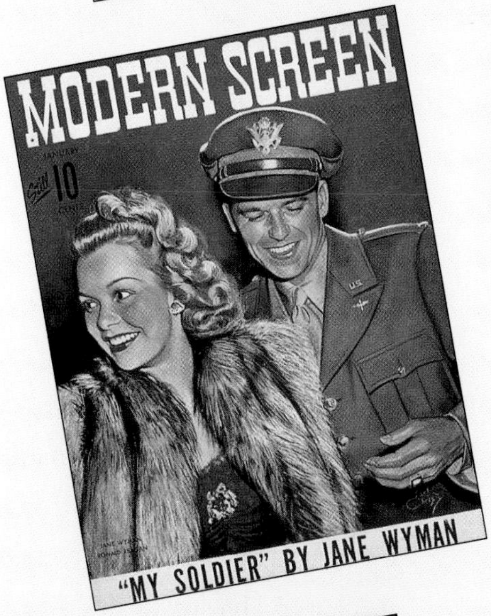

MOVIE-RADIO GUIDE
Exclusive!
Truth About Stars And the Draft
JIMMY STEWART

MODERN SCREEN
Still 10 CENTS
"MY SOLDIER" BY JANE WYMAN

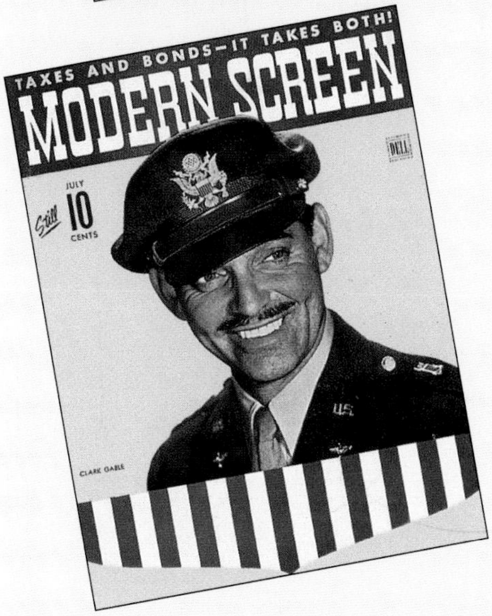

TAXES AND BONDS—IT TAKES BOTH!
MODERN SCREEN
JULY
Still 10 CENTS
DELL
CLARK GABLE

Movie magazines

Rita Hayworth

Betty Grable

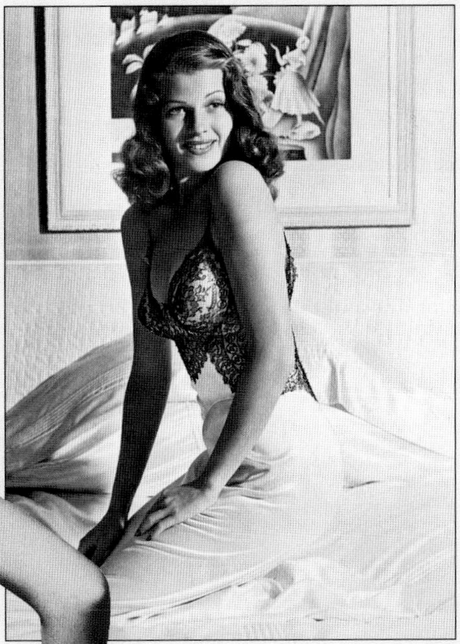

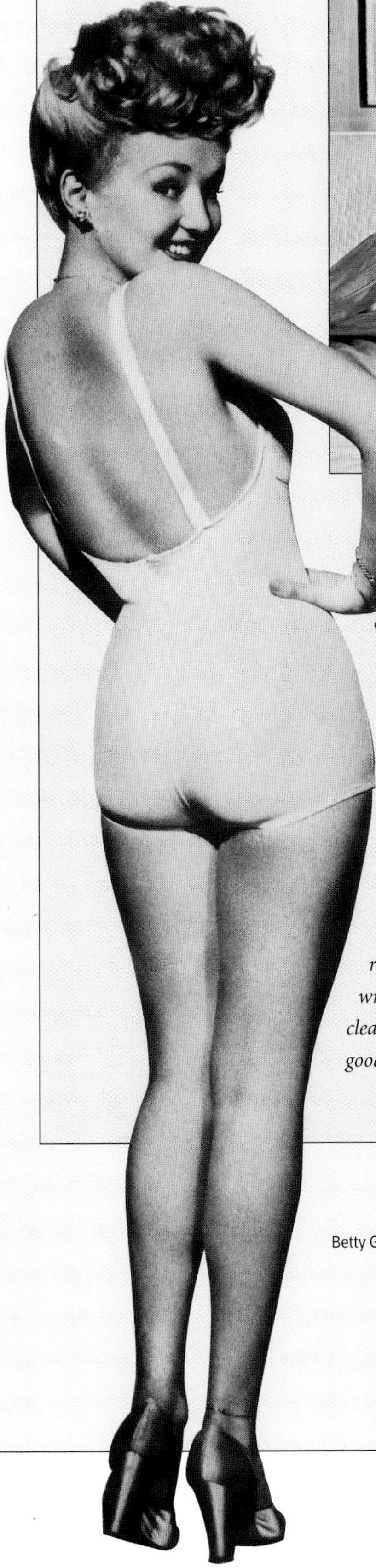

"What We're Fighting For"

Patriotism was one thing, but for many a GI, motivation came in the form of the pinup. Soldiers plastered their lockers, their Quonset huts, and even the insides of their helmets with their favorite shots. Two of the most popular are shown here: Rita Hayworth in a negligee, and Betty Grable showing off her million-dollar legs (Fox publicity had them insured with Lloyds of London). Referring to a running pinup feature in Esquire, one GI wrote, "Those pictures are very much on the clean and healthy side and it gives us guys a good idea of what we're fighting for."

Island Hopping Toward Japan

On the morning of November 20, 1943, as amtracs—amphibious troop carriers with treads—bearing the first wave of Colonel David M. Shoup's Second Marines churned through the lagoon toward tiny Betio Island in the Tarawa Atoll, the tide of the Pacific war had already turned. The fierce naval battles at Coral Sea and Midway and the dogged assault on Guadalcanal had brought Japan's Pacific expansion to a grinding halt, and in September 1943 the enemy set about reinforcing its far-flung island garrisons to form an outer ring of defense against attacks on the Japanese homeland.

American strategy to puncture that ring was a dual thrust: General Douglas MacArthur would push up through the islands of the southwest Pacific while his navy counterpart, Admiral Chester Nimitz, launched an island-hopping drive westward across the central Pacific *(map, right)*. Each was to use the technique of leapfrogging, by which certain strongly defended Japanese garrisons, their supply lines cut, would be skipped and left to wither on the vine. The two forces were to converge south of Japan, within bombing range of the home islands.

The landing on Betio was part of Nimitz's campaign to seize the Gilbert Islands and establish his first central Pacific steppingstone. Just how dug in Japanese forces were became clear as that wave of amtracs trundled onto the coral reef fringing Betio. In preparation for the landing, days of aerial and naval bombardment had blanketed the island with 3,000 tons of high explosive. Nothing could survive such saturation—or so it was thought, until the amtracs came within range of Japanese guns, which began "laying lead to us . . . like holy hell," as one private described it.

Worse was in store for the follow-up troops being transported in Higgins landing craft. Because of an unexpectedly low tide their boats ran aground on the coral reef,

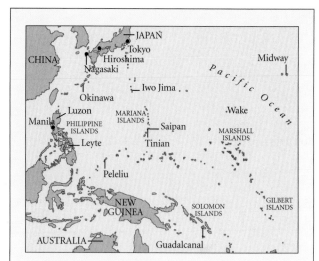

Pacific Progress

July 21, 1942 - January 22, 1943
Papua New Guinea: Allies repulse Japanese overland attempt to take Port Moresby in the southeast.

August 7, 1942 - February 1943
Guadalcanal: U.S. troops rout Japanese and safeguard supply lines to Australia.

June 21, 1943
Central Solomons: U.S. forces land in New Georgia.

November 20, 1943
Gilbert Islands: U.S. landing on Tarawa launches Central Pacific Offensive.

January 31, 1944
Marshall Islands: U.S. forces land on Kwajelein.

April 22, 1944
New Guinea: MacArthur begins final stage of New Guinea campaign with surprise landing on the north coast.

June 15-August 10, 1944
Mariana Islands: U.S. forces take Saipan, Tinian, and Guam.

September 15, 1944
Peleliu: U.S. forces begin one of the bloodiest island campaigns of the Pacific war.

October 20, 1944
Leyte: MacArthur returns to the Philippines.

January 9, 1945
Luzon: MacArthur launches battle for Manila.

February 19, 1945
Iwo Jima: U.S. Marines land and fight the costliest battle in Marine Corps history.

April 1, 1945
Okinawa: Assault landings begin on final steppingstone to Japanese mainland.

Marines advance up the beach on Betio, in the Tarawa Atoll. The island was heavily defended: Bunkers were steel-reinforced concrete pits covered with up to 10 feet of coral sand. Many Japanese who didn't succumb to the assault committed suicide.

and many men were fated to slosh half a mile to shore through a hail of mortar and machine-gun fire. For 30 hours the marines were mowed down, a moving target of human flesh. By the second day, Betio's blue lagoon was a gruesome junkyard of blasted landing craft and bloody corpses.

Clearly, too much had been expected of the preinvasion bombing. "A million men cannot take Tarawa in a hundred years," the garrison's commander, Admiral Kaiji Shibasaki, had boasted. The cause of his optimism was a veritable fortress: 500 concrete-and-steel pillboxes, bombproof bunkers, a spider web of tunnels and trenches, a coconut-log sea wall and, offshore, mines, concrete pyramids, and barbed wire arranged to funnel boats and wading men into the direct path of Japanese fire. Defending this outpost were some 4,800 men, most of whom had vowed to fight to the death.

Unfortunately for the advancing marines, Betio would have to be taken at close range, pillbox by pillbox, with hand grenades and demolition charges tossed into narrow firing slits. For many the prospect was daunting. Some men had to be kicked into action; others were roused by the pluck of lone heroes. The redoubtable Colonel Shoup, wounded but still fighting, ran into one of his officers hunkered down behind some coral rubble. "Where's your squad?" Shoup inquired. "Wiped out," the officer said. "Well then," bellowed Shoup, "get yourself another one!"

Seventy-six hours after they first hit the shore, the marines managed to prevail. Victory was dear: 1,056 Americans dead and 2,292 wounded in one of the greatest concentrations of casualties of World War II. Back home, Americans were shocked that so much blood had been shed for a small chunk of coral. Grieving parents who had believed that Japan could be bombed out of the war flooded Nimitz with letters blaming him for the fiasco. The lessons of Betio were soon learned: Less than three months later the Americans hopped over to the Marshalls and took more than 30 of its islands at a cost of only 594 men.

Nimitz's next steppingstone was to be the Marianas, a short 1,270 miles from Tokyo. Their capture would do what Japan had dreaded: breach its inner ring of defense. Steadily, with General MacArthur probing the north coast of New Guinea for a springboard to the Philippines, the two offensive thrusts were closing in on Japan's jugular.

While clearing corpses from a cave on Saipan, a marine finds a miracle: an infant, bloody but alive. Saipan marked the breaching of Japan's inner ring of defense. Dug into its mountainous spine were 29,662 defenders, including many desperate civilians who after the battle flung themselves into the sea from Saipan's jagged northern cliffs.

A Code They Couldn't Break

Pacific commanders realized early in the war that the Japanese had broken U.S. secret codes and were deciphering vital military communications. A foolproof system was needed. But instead of turning to experts in cryptography, the marines placed their faith in a people whose language few others understood: the Navajo. Thirty Navajo marine recruits created a code based on their native vocabulary, using words they could easily associate with military terms. Thus, a bomber plane was "jay-sho" (buzzard); bombs were "a-ye-shi" (eggs).

The Navajo code talkers hit beaches from Guadalcanal to Okinawa (the men above were on Bougainville), sending messages with amazing speed and accuracy between command post and field. And the enemy could not translate or easily stop them. "Sometimes we had to crawl, had to run, had to lie partly submerged in a swamp . . . pinned under fire," said one code talker. "We transmitted our messages under any and all conditions."

Letters Home

They were a lifeline for servicemen in every theater of the war, a connection to a world where bombs didn't fall and bullets didn't fly. And in many ways, the letters troops wrote were just as important for maintaining those ties as the ones they received.

So it was for PFC Henry Kagan, a member of the engineering corps that followed the marines into Saipan. Henry had been called up in 1943 and would serve for almost three years, during which time he wrote to his beloved wife, Bella, at least once every single day. He told her about everything he was going through and poured out his longing to be back home. He was especially keen that Bella save his letters. She did. And Henry did come home. The letters were put away in a trunk—a treasure unearthed decades later by their youngest son, this book's managing editor.

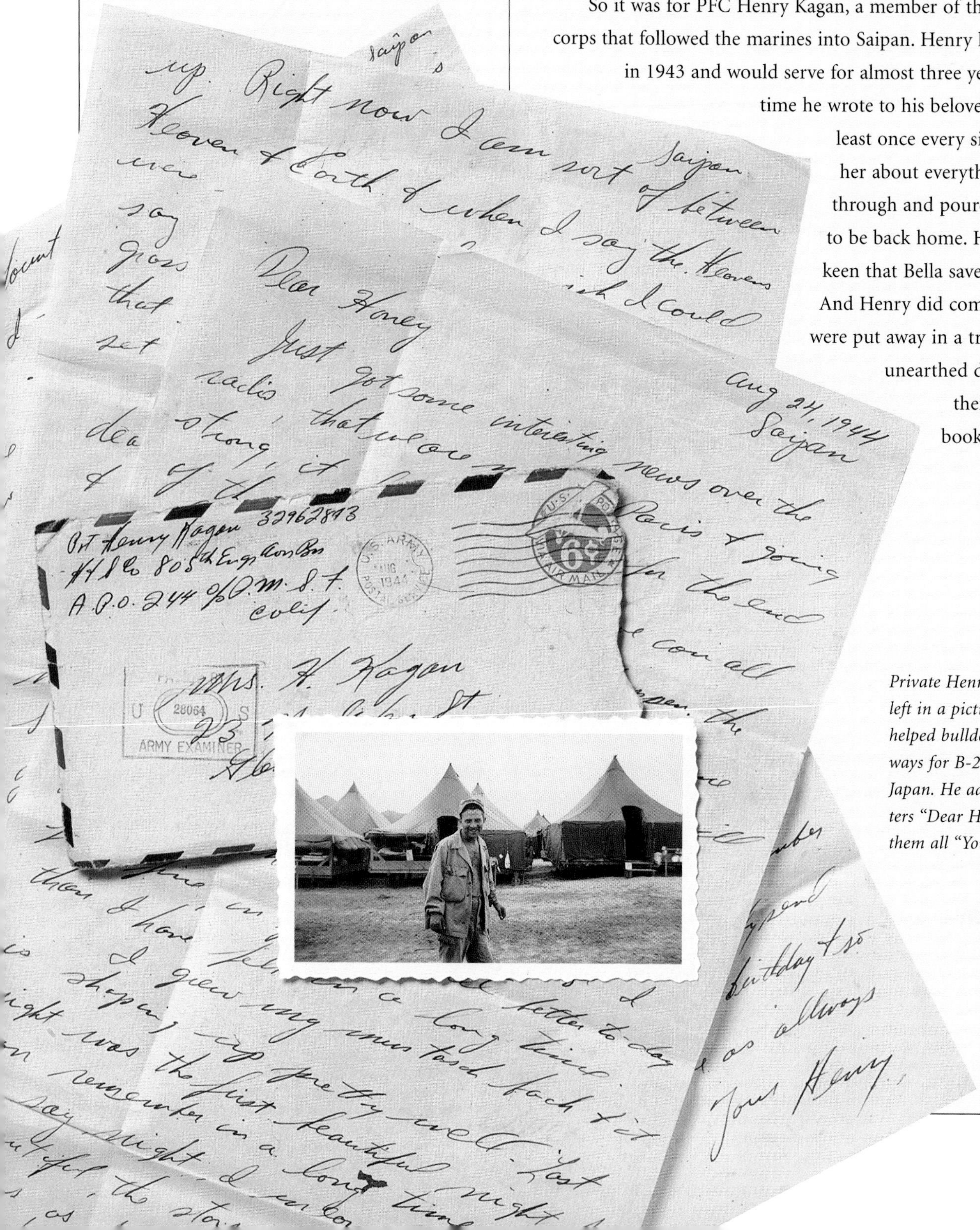

Private Henry Kagan, shown at left in a picture taken on Saipan, helped bulldoze coral to make runways for B-29s that would bomb Japan. He addressed all of his letters "Dear Honey" and signed them all "Your Henry."

Aug. 24, 1944
Saipan

Dear Honey

Just got some interesting news over the radio, that we are now in Paris and going strong. It looks very close for the end of the European war. Then we can all look for big things to happen. The end of this whole war will come soon after that. I think there will be peace on Earth and I will be coming home to you and our son . . .

I grew my mustache back and it is shaping up pretty well. Last night was the first beautiful night I can remember in a long time. When I say night, I mean the sky was beautiful, the stars were shining in the heavens as I lay in my cot looking upward, and that is the only way I want to go through life, with my head up. Right now I am sort of between Heaven and Earth and when I say the Heavens were beautiful I also wish I could say the Earth was also beautiful, the grass and the mountains etc. But I'm afraid that beautiful day won't come until I set foot on good old U.S. soil.

I think I have changed a great deal. I believe in the right things and I fight for what is right, and I will admit I'm wrong. Also you might be interested in knowing I have sworn, that night, that horrible night when we first set foot on Saipan and I was awakened by a roar of a Jap motor and a tremendous burst of bombs all around me, I crawled out of my pup tent like a scared rabbit, my teeth were chattering and my knees were shaking and my eyes were three times their size. I was so scared I didn't know where to go, not having a foxhole. I started to dig with my hands and feet. The sweat was rolling off me like a fountain. I was in a daze. I was ready and I thought, that was the end. I prayed and prayed to God and asked him to forgive me for all my sins and I swore if I ever got home alive and safe I would never gamble again and as much as I like to gamble, that is my promise. Just as soon as I step on home ground.

You may not believe this but it is true, every word of it.

This is just a little chapter of my experience on Saipan Island.

By the way I meant to ask you, do you save these letters? I hope so!

Here is hoping for a wonderful New Year. Being as my mind, or rather these days I find it hard to remember dates, like Birthdays, etc. Kindly send me the correct dates of your birthday and so on. Answer soon.

Love as always,
Your Henry

Bella Kagan sent Henry this picture of herself and their firstborn, Leonard, in July 1944. Henry kept these and other shots in his helmet during the invasion of Saipan. "I think they brought me luck," he wrote.

"By the way I meant to ask you, do you save these letters? I hope so!"

Henry Kagan, August 24, 1944

Teen idol Frank Sinatra, with his silken voice and intimate delivery, gazes intensely at his audience during a concert. Ushers sometimes had to revive swooning fans with smelling salts.

Arts and Entertainment

The Broadway hit Oklahoma!, a love story set in cattle country at the turn of the century, blended a folksy score and lyrics with modern dance.

As America's taste in music moved from big-band swing to solo vocalists, the king of crooners was Frank Sinatra (left). His first solo performance at New York's Paramount Ballroom on December 30, 1942, erupted into a frenzy of teenage squeals and an occasional faint. "He was a skinny kid with big ears," said bandleader Tommy Dorsey, "and yet what he did to women was something awful." Sinatra had his first million-selling hit, "All or Nothing at All," in 1943.

A few blocks away, Rodgers and Hammerstein's groundbreaking musical Oklahoma! (above) dispensed with stars, chorus girls, and sight gags, instead focusing on a romantic story line dramatized through song and dance. Its opening in March changed the complexion of musical theater forever.

Popular books of the year were Guadalcanal Diary, which faithfully reported on the 1942 battle, and the coming-of-age tale A Tree Grows in Brooklyn.

1944
★
The Turning Point

At the beginning of 1944, the Allies found out why no other army had ever invaded southern Italy and attempted to make its way up the narrow peninsula. Italy's mountainous backbone overwhelmingly favored the defenders, and the gifted German commander, Field Marshal Albert Kesselring, had taken good advantage of the terrain. Midway between Naples and Rome, he had created a band of steel-reinforced concrete bunkers, minefields, and other fortifications across the peninsula's waist. This "Gustav Line" was anchored near its southwest end by Monte Cassino, a 1,700-foot-high chunk of rock that commanded both the town of Cassino (*left*) and Route 6, the only feasible road to Rome. There, four months after the successful landings in the south, the Allied advance bogged down behind the Rapido River.

The Allies first tried an end run around the western flank of the Gustav Line. On January 22, hoping to divert the Germans from their mountain strongholds, 40,000 U.S. troops landed near Anzio, a seaside resort west of Cassino. But instead of striking swiftly inland to cut off the German rear, the Americans paused for nine days to consolidate their beachhead. The Germans, acting on Hitler's personal orders to lance this "abscess," quickly moved in divisions from France, Germany, and Yugoslavia. Counterattacking with heavy artillery that included "Anzio

Smoke rises from the ruins of Cassino after the lethal Allied bombardment—1,100 tons of bombs and 196,000 artillery shells—on March 15, 1944. Wedged between the mountains and the Rapido River, the town and the heavily fortified Monte Cassino looming above it farther west blocked the road to Rome.

With two of his division commanders perched in the back, Lieutenant General Mark Clark rides in triumph through American-liberated Rome on June 4, 1944. In the background is Saint Peter's Basilica and Vatican City.

An American soldier shares his rations with an Italian infant. Such gestures caused the Italians to welcome the Americans as liberators.

Annie"—an enormous railway gun capable of hurling 560-pound shells nearly 40 miles—they nearly drove the Americans back into the sea. "I had hoped we were hurling a wildcat onto the shore," said Winston Churchill, "but all we got was a stranded whale."

The Allies now had to assault the Gustav Line to relieve the pressure on the GIs barely hanging on at Anzio. For nearly four months, they hammered away at Cassino and the mountains flanking it. Burdened by Italy's harshest winter in decades, the men fought in numbing cold and knee-deep mud and snow. Unable to dig foxholes for cover in the stony ground, they had to claw their way up the icy cliffs in the open, dodging flying splinters of rock as well as murderous enemy fire.

Allied air power was devastating, but sometimes it backfired. German artillery on Monte Cassino was so deadly that the Allies mistakenly concluded the enemy must have stationed spotters in the sixth-century Benedictine monastery crowning it. Only after U.S. bombers reduced the famous monastery to ruins, setting off a worldwide protest, did the Germans actually move in and take up nearly impregnable positions amid the heaps of rubble. Waves of bombers then demolished the town of Cassino, but created craters so large that the tanks of the attacking New Zealanders could not make it through to support the infantry.

On May 11, for their fourth major attack on the Gustav Line, the Allies massed more than 15 divisions along a 25-mile front. Deafening salvos from more than 1,600 guns signaled the launch of an assault by troops of several Allied nations. French-led Moroccan Goumiers, sure-footed in their flimsy sandals, clambered up peaks of the 5,000-foot-high mountains southwest of Cassino that no one else thought could be scaled. Packing their supplies on mules, they knifed through the enemy defenses, then turned right and threatened the German rear. The British, meanwhile, also outflanked Cassino, and members of the Polish II Corps took Monte Cassino unopposed, raising their flag over the ruined monastery.

The Germans should have been caught as they withdrew to the north. But British-American rivalry interfered again. Instead of cutting off the German retreat, the ambitious U.S. commander, Lieutenant General Mark Clark, decided to push for Rome to beat the British there. On June 4, 1944, Clark and his Americans entered the Eternal City to a tumultuous reception from its residents. The road from the Rapido River to Rome had cost the Allies five months and 105,000 casualties.

Clark's decision to hurry to Rome—a city of symbolic significance but of no strategic value—allowed most of the retreating Germans to

"Now that ya mention it, Joe, it does sound like th' patter of rain on a tin roof."

A Comic Look at GI Life

The unofficial spokesman for the American infantryman was a puckish GI named Bill Mauldin *(above),* who drew cartoons for the army newspaper *Stars and Stripes.* Mauldin's most famous characters were Willie and Joe *(right, top and bottom),* scragglebearded dogfaces who sweated and shivered in foxholes and griped about food, MPs, and rearechelon "brass hats." Higher-ups chafed at Mauldin's depictions, but soldiers loved them; they helped take the edge off the GIs' own misery.

"You'll get over it, Joe. Oncet I wuz gonna write a book exposin' the army after th' war myself."

Hunkering down near one of their P-51 Mustangs, pilots of the 332nd Fighter Group talk over a mission at their base at Rametelli, Italy. Because these Tuskegee Airmen painted the tails of their planes vermilion, the grateful bomber crews they protected called them Red Tail Angels.

escape. In the mountains of northern Italy, Kesselring established yet another formidable defensive line across the peninsula. The dogged fighting for this new barrier would go on until nearly the end of the war.

"The best of shepherds." Behind the front lines in Italy, the Americans had established air bases from which to strike deep into Hitler's Europe. The new long-range fighter escorts made this possible again, as they had for the bombers flying from England *(pages 90-91)*. No fighter group proved more effective than the 332nd, the all-black unit trained at Tuskegee, Alabama. Under the hard-driving command of Colonel Benjamin O. Davis Sr., the century's first black graduate of West Point, the four squadrons of Tuskegee Airmen flew the long-range P-47 Thunderbolts and P-51 Mustangs that made possible repeated pounding of production facilities in Germany and eastern Europe. Unlike many escorts, they stayed with their bombers all through the attack, winning the praise of one pilot as "the best of shepherds." Not a single bomber they escorted was lost to an enemy fighter—a record unmatched by any unit with as many missions.

"We fought two wars, one with the enemy and the other back home in the U.S.A."

Tuskegee Airman Louis Purnell

D-Day

His orders were to "enter the continent of Europe and . . . undertake operations aimed at the heart of Germany and the destruction of her armed forces." To this end, General Dwight David Eisenhower—Allied supreme commander—had assembled in England the mightiest invasion armada in history: 175,000 assault troops, 5,000 vessels of every type, 20,000 vehicles, and 11,000 aircraft. He had worked 20 hours a day to prepare his men and calm his contentious generals with the help of the infectious grin that was said to be worth 20 divisions. He had gambled that the storm raging over the English Channel would break on Tuesday, June 6, 1944—and had taken personal responsibility if everything failed.

Now, on the eve of D-Day—the long-awaited invasion of western Europe—he knew his forces were "tense as a coiled spring." As he bade good luck to the 101st Airborne Division, the 53-year-old commander everyone referred to as Ike spoke with the humility of a kid from Kansas. "I've done all I can," he told a paratrooper. "Now it's up to you."

The objective was a 60-mile arc of beaches in Normandy on the northern coast of France. During the night, U.S. and

On the eve of the Normandy invasion, General Eisenhower chats with paratroopers of the 101st Airborne Division at their base in England. "Now quit worrying, General," one of them called out. "We'll take care of this thing for you."

British airborne forces swooped in by parachute and glider to provide a protective shield at either end of this planned beachhead. Then the seaborne forces approached Normandy shortly after dawn. To soften up the German defenses, Allied guns on battleships, cruisers, and destroyers unleashed salvo after salvo, and hundreds of bombers pounded the shore. Only then did the first wave of assault troops, crammed into flat-bottomed landing craft, prepare to go ashore at H-Hour—6:30 a.m.

"Soldiers, Sailors and Airmen . . . You are about to embark upon the Great Crusade."

Eisenhower's orders to the troops for D-Day

On the Allied left, the British and Canadian forces landed with only moderate opposition on the three eastern beaches—code-named Gold, Juno, and Sword. On the far right, at the westernmost Utah Beach, the vanguard of the U.S. Fourth Division jumped into waist-deep water and went ashore under the command of Brigadier General Theodore Roosevelt, the eldest son of one president and cousin of the current one. The only general in the first wave and the oldest man in the invasion, Roosevelt had an arthritic shoulder and a bad heart, which would cost him his life five weeks later. But on this historic day, armed with a pistol, a walking stick, and a penchant for

commanding by example, he inspired his seasick rookies to push inland and link up with their airborne comrades.

The scene of the fiercest fighting was Omaha Beach, a four-mile crescent east of Utah. Ranks of steel, wooden, and concrete obstacles guarded the water's edge, and scores of concrete-lined pillboxes and other fortifications studded the steep cliffs and bluffs overlooking the beach.

The artillery, mortars, and machine guns in these strong-points hammered the assault troops with a relentless cross fire; two-thirds of the first wave were shot down in the churning surf. All but seven or eight members of one 197-man company were killed or wounded within 10 minutes of landing on the beach.

By 9:00 a.m. the situation was critical. Omaha was so

Leaving behind their landing craft, GIs laden with combat gear wade toward obstacle-lined Omaha Beach on D-Day. German defenders on the bluffs beyond poured machine-gun and mortar fire upon the invaders. Soon, said Sergeant Robert Slaughter of the 116th Infantry Regiment, there were "dead men floating in the water and there were live men acting dead."

hopelessly clogged with human bodies and mechanical debris that hundreds of boats waiting to land circled offshore "like a stampeding herd of cattle," in the words of one observer. A dozen miles offshore, the commander of the U.S. contingent, Lieutenant General Omar Bradley, considered calling off the attack on Omaha and transferring the follow-up troops to the British beaches.

Even as Bradley debated with himself, however, commanders were rallying their demoralized troops. Colonel Charles Canham, commander of the 29th Division's 116th Regiment, with his wounded right hand in a sling and a pistol clutched in his left hand, screamed for his officers to "get the hell off this damn beach and go kill some Germans." Small groups began to inch up the

bluffs, supported by destroyers that moved in so close to shell the German strongpoints that they scraped bottom. The GIs were on Omaha to stay—at a cost of one-third of the Allies' 9,000 casualties that day.

Buildup and Slowdown. In the days after the invasion, while U.S. and British forces expanded and connected their separate beachheads, the Allies began an enormous buildup of men and matériel. To create sheltered water for docking and unloading ships, a pair of artificial harbors were assembled off the beaches from more than 600 steel and concrete sections towed piecemeal from England. Sailors also proved surprisingly adept at running the big landing craft known as LSTs right up on the beach to disgorge cargo. As on D-Day, all this occurred with no threat from the Luftwaffe, which remained in Germany trying to defend the homeland from Allied bombers. By the end of June, three weeks after D-Day, the Allies had put ashore one million men, a half million tons of supplies, and more than 175,000 vehicles.

Logistically on schedule, the Allied forces nevertheless lagged far behind their tactical timetable. For six

The day after D-Day at Omaha Beach (top), reinforcements of the U.S. Second Division head inland toward the fighting. At right, Omaha swarms with ships and trucks bringing in ever more men and matériel. Barrage balloons guarded against low-flying enemy aircraft, which rarely put in an appearance.

In Normandy, GIs search a hedgerow for enemy snipers who already have claimed one of their comrades. Hedgerows occurred every few hundred feet, hemming in small fields. With their heaped-up earthen mounds sprouting thickets of foliage, they proved to be ideal terrain for the German defenders.

weeks the British on the eastern flank were stymied in front of Caen, an objective they were supposed to have captured on D-Day. Only eight miles inland, Caen blocked the open road to Paris, and the Germans concentrated most of their tanks there. On the western flank, it took the Americans nearly three weeks to capture the port of Cherbourg, on the peninsula northwest of the beaches. Then they moved south toward the key crossroads of Saint-Lô, but at an excruciatingly slow pace.

What slowed the Americans as much as anything was the French countryside itself, a patchwork of thousands of small fields enclosed by virtually impenetrable hedgerows dating from Roman times. The hedgerows, built to mark boundaries and keep in cattle, consisted of earthen mounds up to four feet in thickness and height,

crowned with dense thickets of thornbushes and trees. Behind almost every one, dug in at the base with mortars and machine guns that fired 1,200 rounds a minute, were German defenders. Light American Sherman tanks attempting to climb the hedgerows exposed their unarmored bellies and became easy targets for the German *Panzerfaust,* a type of bazooka.

Tackling the hedgerows required new tactics and mechanical ingenuity. The Americans developed small assault teams: a squad of riflemen supported by a mortar, a machine gun, and explosives experts. To plow through the thick foliage, tankers welded pointed steel plates on the front of their vehicles. Because the plates looked like horns, tanks thus outfitted became known as rhinos. Even with such innovations, a team could make it through

An American gun crew in the full cry of battle fires its howitzer at retreating Germans near the Normandy town of Carentan. Capture of this vital crossroads eight miles inland on June 12 allowed the linkup of U.S. troops from the Utah and Omaha beachheads.

only a couple of hedgerows a day, perhaps a tenth of a mile. So many casualties resulted that one medic calculated every hedgerow cost 32 grains of morphine. It was July 18 before the Americans negotiated this lethal obstacle course and took Saint-Lô, only 15 miles inland.

A week later, a major bombardment—including nearly 5,000 tons of bombs and 125,000 artillery shells—

cracked open the front near Saint-Lô. Tanks poured through an area so devastated that one German general thought it looked "like the face of the moon." Reinforced by the Third Army under Lieutenant General George Patton, the Americans sped eastward at up to 40 miles a day.

In mid-August, the Allies took advantage of their superior mobility to partially trap the retreating Germans. The British drove south from Caen while Patton's tanks turned north, aiming to close the pocket. Two-fifths of the 100,000 Germans trapped there escaped eastward through a gap near the town of Falaise. The remainder were shot down or captured.

Winning Normandy led to the liberation of France, and on August 25, Free French armored forces entered Paris. Their arrival, with U.S. infantry close behind, touched off a tumultuous celebration by people who had endured more than four years of German occupation.

> "I have seen the faces of young people in love and the faces of old people at peace with their God. I have never seen in any face such joy as radiated from the faces of the people of Paris this morning."
>
> *Time* correspondent Charles C. Wertenbaker

Troops of the U.S. 28th Infantry Division march through the Arc de Triomphe and down the Champs Élysées in a victory parade four days after the liberation of Paris. For military reasons, Eisenhower had intended to bypass Paris and then liberate it in September, but political pressures forced him to allow Free French forces to enter the city on August 25.

Japan's Leyte Gamble

When U.S. troops invaded the central Philippines on October 20, 1944, the Japanese seized upon a desperate scheme to turn the tide in the Pacific. The plan called for mustering three separate task forces from the shrinking Imperial Navy: a decoy to lure away one of the two American fleets supporting the landing on the island of Leyte; and two other groups, the Central and Southern Forces, to converge upon the remaining U.S. fleet and destroy it. The decision to take this gamble—described by Japan's top admiral as being "as difficult as swallowing molten iron"—brought on the greatest sea battle of all time.

The Battle for Leyte Gulf began on October 24. Carrier-based planes from the powerful U.S. Third Fleet attacked the Central Force, focusing on the *Yamato* and the *Musashi*, the world's biggest battleships. For five hours they pounded both ships, finally sinking the *Musashi* with direct hits of 17 torpedoes and 19 bombs. When the Japanese reversed course, the U.S. commander, Admiral William "Bull" Halsey, assumed they were beaten. He steamed impetuously northward to pursue

---

As the stricken Japanese carrier Zuikaku rolls over, crewmen raise their arms in a farewell banzai cheer. Nearly half the 1,700-man crew went down with the ship, which was part of the decoy force that lured the U.S. Third Fleet from Leyte Gulf.

A month after the Battle for Leyte Gulf, firefighters on the U.S. carrier Intrepid battle blazes caused when two kamikaze pilots deliberately crashed their planes. Its navy shattered at Leyte, Japan turned more and more to such desperation suicide missions.

"I shall fall like a blossom from a radiant cherry tree."

Kamikaze pilot Isao Matsuo

the enemy decoy force, leaving the northern approach to Leyte Gulf unguarded.

Before dawn the next day, the U.S. Seventh Fleet under Admiral Thomas Kinkaid intercepted the enemy Southern Force and executed a classic maneuver, known as crossing the T, to block the southern approach to Leyte Gulf and then smash the 12-ship flotilla. Only then did Kinkaid realize that Halsey had taken off. To guard the rest of the gulf he had only six slow escort carriers—old merchant ships fitted with short flight decks—and seven smaller ships with a mere 29 guns.

But when the remnants of the Japanese Central Force entered the gulf from the north, the U.S. contingent put on a good show. Rear Admiral Clifton Sprague launched every plane and had his outgunned ships throw up smoke screens. After more than two hours of fighting—including attacks by kamikaze suicide pilots, a new strategy employed by the Japanese —the enemy turned away. Sprague had thrown the Japanese into such confusion they thought they were facing Halsey's mighty Third Fleet. Halsey in fact was only then rushing back in response to frantic radio calls for help after wiping out Japan's last four carriers.

The Japanese had lost the battle—26 of their warships sunk to six for the Americans—and in the process had crippled their navy beyond repair.

Crewmen of the USS Intrepid crowd the rail for a mass burial at sea of comrades killed during kamikaze attacks. Bodies were rarely, if ever, returned home.

The Last Blitzkrieg

O nly Hitler thought it would work. His own generals considered it too ambitious. The Allied generals didn't believe the battered Germans were even capable of mounting such an offensive. But Hitler cherished the memory of 1940, when his armies had smashed through Belgium's Ardennes Forest and routed the French.

During the autumn of 1944, as the Allies closed in on Germany, the Führer prepared a new blitzkrieg in the Ardennes. Along the German border, facing the thinly held Allied front in Belgium and Luxembourg, he assembled a force of more than 250,000 men with nearly 1,000 tanks and assault guns. He intended to burst through westward to the Meuse River, split the enemy armies, and then seize the critical port of Antwerp. Preparations went forward in the greatest secrecy, and the Allies—lulled by their successes of the past six months—suspected nothing.

At dawn on December 16, the Germans struck. After a 2,000-gun bombardment, infantry wearing white camouflage rushed forward through the fog and snow. Behind them rumbled phalanxes of armor,

GIs surrender to officers of the First SS Panzer Division during the first few days of the German offensive in the Ardennes Forest. The Germans captured more than 7,000 Americans—and executed at least 350 of them in cold blood.

"This battle is to decide whether we shall live or die. . . . The battle must be fought with brutality, and all the resistance must be broken in a wave of terror. The enemy must be beaten—now or never! Thus lives our Germany."

Adolf Hitler, December 11, 1944, before the Battle of the Bulge

Members of the Second Infantry Division take cover in a snowy ditch during shelling on the second day of the German offensive. Though surprised by the sudden attacks, these and many other GIs stayed put long enough to slow the enemy momentum.

including the big 60-ton Tiger tanks, unhindered by U.S. aircraft grounded during the foul weather. The attack covered a 50-mile front, and everywhere the 83,000 American defenders were outnumbered. In some places the ratio was 10 to 1, and these GIs were simply overwhelmed. Here and there, a squad or platoon of defenders managed to hold out for a time in farmhouses or frozen foxholes, taking huge casualties while slowing the German onslaught.

But panic seized many U.S. units filled with raw replacements. Their confusion was compounded by 150 members of a special German brigade who roamed the rear dressed in U.S. and British uniforms. Selected because they spoke idiomatic English, they drove captured jeeps, trucks, or tanks and sowed disorder behind the lines by spreading rumors and changing road signs. On the fourth day of the German offensive, more than 7,000 GIs, most of them newly arrived draftees, found themselves surrounded and forced to surrender. Farther north, 350 captured Americans were gunned down by an elite Nazi SS panzer division; at least 86 of them were executed in an open field near Malmédy. Word of the "Malmédy Massacre" galvanized angry Americans all along the collapsing front.

Exhaustion shows on the face of a GI during the siege of Bastogne. The defenders—from several different divisions—found camaraderie in their plight, calling themselves the Battered Bastards of Bastogne.

The Germans soon punched a dent in the Allied lines up to 65 miles deep. At their furthest penetration, they reached within four miles of the Meuse. But the Americans, by holding firm on the northern and southern flanks, managed to squeeze the German thrusts into a salient only 45 miles across at its widest point. The shape of the salient provided the conflict's famous name—the Battle of the Bulge.

Within the bulge, two road junctions 30 miles apart proved vital. The Americans stalled the Germans by holding the northern crossroads, Saint-Vith, for five days before pulling back. In the southern sector, the 101st Airborne Division arrived to reinforce the town of Bastogne on December 19 just before the Germans got there. The Germans quickly surrounded the town. But the most direct route to the Meuse ran right through Bastogne, and their panzer columns backed up at this bottleneck. On December 22, the German commander sent

En route to relieve Bastogne, a tank crew of George Patton's Third Army pauses to watch as transport planes prepare to parachute supplies to the town's beleaguered defenders.

"This time the Kraut has stuck his head in a meat grinder. And this time I've got hold of the handle."

General George S. Patton, December 19, 1944

emissaries to demand Bastogne's surrender. The one-word reply of the 101st's acting commander, Brigadier General Anthony McAuliffe, went down in history as a resounding "Nuts!"

On Christmas Day, the GIs delivered their own message. They knocked out 18 German tanks that had managed to crash through the perimeter. The next day, an armored spearhead from Patton's Third Army broke through from the south to lift the siege. The failure to take Bastogne doomed the German offensive, though the bulge would not be fully eliminated until mid-January. The battle was the U.S. Army's largest single action of the war and resulted in 81,000 American casualties. Enemy losses amounted to 120,000—a toll Hitler could ill afford when the Allies struck into the German heartland in the new year.

Generals Bradley, Eisenhower, and Patton (left to right) confer in Bastogne after the siege. Patton was chomping at the bit to lead the next Allied offensive across the Rhine deep into Germany.

At the Movies

Hollywood's take on the war ran a wide gamut, from psychological dramas such as Alfred Hitchcock's *Lifeboat (left)* to Disney cartoon spoofs *(far right)*. By 1944, actual wartime events were making it to the screen. One of the most popular dramatizations was *Thirty Seconds Over Tokyo (above, left)*, a fictionalized version of Colonel James Doolittle's daring 1942 bombing of Japan *(pages 60-61)*, starring Spencer Tracy as Doolittle.

Mickey Rooney and Elizabeth Taylor share a moment in National Velvet. Taylor was only 12 at the time; 24-year-old Rooney joined the army soon after the film's release.

★ 1944

Arts and Entertainment

While nostalgia held sway in films like *National Velvet* (*opposite*)—the heartwarming story of a girl and her horse—and Judy Garland's *Meet Me in St. Louis* (*below*), real women were trying some less-than-traditional roles in professional sports. The draft had continued to deprive baseball of its best players, so Chicago Cubs owner Philip K. Wrigley had started the All-American Girls Professional Baseball League in 1943; by 1944 it was in full swing. Ground rules for the players included wearing dresses and makeup on the field and attending charm school in their off-hours. "I never thought about if I was good or bad. I just loved playing ball," recalled Dottie Schroeder, one of the first 60 players in the league.

Dorothy Kamenshek of the Rockford Peaches (above), considered by some to be the best all-around player in the women's league, makes a midair catch. Former Yankee Wally Pipp called her "the fanciest-fielding first baseman I've ever seen, man or woman."

Meet Me in St. Louis (right) helped seven-year-old Margaret O'Brien win a special Oscar, and featured Judy Garland singing classics like "The Boy Next Door" and "Have Yourself a Merry Little Christmas." Only Gone With the Wind had earned MGM more money.

On February 10, 1942, Glenn Miller received a gold record (right)—the first ever presented to a recording artist—for selling a million copies of "Chattanooga Choo-Choo." Miller's trademark trombone (below) replaced his first instrument—the mandolin.

Glen Miller's Special Sound

Swing music was all the rage in the war years, and one of the most popular bandleaders was Glenn Miller, a trombonist whose greater claim to fame was as an arranger. A perfectionist, Miller shunned improvisational, solo-oriented swing for precise arrangements, smoothing out swing's jazzier elements and adding a dash of romantic balladeering. The result was distinctive and soon became known as the Miller sound.

In the fall of 1942, Miller was 38 years old. He was married, a father, and his eyes were bad. As one commentator put it, he could have avoided the draft until the German army reached Chicago. But Miller, like so many others, wanted to do his part, and so he enlisted in the army. What his role should be was obvious to everyone, and he soon had assembled several bands. His first army gigs were stateside and included playing swing versions of Sousa marches for training drills. By 1944, Miller's Army Air Force Orchestra was performing in Britain and making up to 17 broadcasts a week over the Armed Forces Network.

But Miller was itching to get to the front-line troops. On December 15, he and two others set off in a small plane for Paris to arrange an appearance there. They never made it. On Christmas Day, the New York Times announced that Miller's plane was missing and that no trace of it had been found. None ever was.

"I, like every patriotic American, have an obligation to fulfill. That obligation is to lend as much support as I can to winning the war."

Glenn Miller, September 1942

Captain Glenn Miller and his band perform for 1,500 servicemen—some clinging from the rafters—at an air base in Halesworth, England, in 1944. Miller believed that "America means freedom and there's no expression of freedom quite so sincere as music."

Returning to the Philippines a second time, General Douglas MacArthur strides ashore at Luzon toward photographers and a throng of Filipinos cheering from the beach. It was an encore of his triumphant landing at Leyte 80 days previously.

1945

★

Days of Victory

It was the war's most famous vow. "I shall return," General Douglas MacArthur had told the people of the Philippines when he was forced to leave on March 11, 1942. And return he did—twice, in fact. He went ashore during the invasion of Leyte Island on October 20, 1944. Then, with his flair for the dramatic, he repeated the gesture on January 9, 1945, wading onto the beach two hours after the initial assaults on Luzon, the Philippines' main island.

His Sixth Army moved swiftly down Luzon to secure two of the main strategic goals: Clark Field, the huge air base, and Manila Bay, a possible launching point for the anticipated invasion of Japan. MacArthur also sent a column racing ahead to the capital, Manila, to free 3,700 interned American  civilians. Then a combined air-sea assault seized Corregidor—the tiny but heavily fortified island at the mouth of Manila Bay, where U.S. troops had held out tenaciously before surrendering in May 1942.

But the battle for Manila itself became a month-long nightmare. Fighting raged from building to building, and Filipino civilians got caught in the cross fire. Some

Aboard the transport President Hayes docked at San Francisco, sailors coming home after being wounded in the Pacific catch up on the news of the Luzon invasion (inset).

100,000 of them were killed—six for every combatant who died. In the mountainous north of Luzon, the Japanese held on even more resolutely, tying down four U.S. divisions until near the end of the war.

Inferno on Iwo Jima. The island was tiny, an eight-square-mile chunk of volcanic rock and ash, but it happened to be in the right place. Iwo Jima stood only 660 miles south of Tokyo, and it was considered vital to a stepping up of the air war against Japan: B-29 Superfortresses flying from Saipan farther south needed airfields for emergency landings and forward bases for their P-51 fighter escorts.

U.S. ships and planes gave Iwo the heaviest preinvasion pounding of the Pacific war. But when the first of 70,000 marines landed on February 19, sinking to their shins in volcanic ash, they found the enemy virtually unscathed. Some 21,000 defenders were holed up in a labyrinth of bunkers, pillboxes, and caves connected by 11 miles of tunnels. The marines clawed their way to the 550-foot summit of Mount Suribachi on the fifth day, raising the American flag in the most famous photograph of the war *(cover)*. It took them a month more to root out an enemy so fanatical that only 216 would surrender. Iwo was the most costly operation in Marine Corps history, claiming the lives of 6,821 leathernecks.

Even before the entire island was won, the first crippled B-29 made an emergency landing on Iwo. In all, some 2,400 damaged Superfortresses—carrying 27,000 crewmen—would land safely on this volcanic waste so dearly bought.

On Iwo Jima, marines armed with flamethrowers set ablaze the entrance to an enemy cave. Bunkers, concrete blockhouses, and underground fortifications bristled with more than 800 Japanese gun emplacements that had to be cleared one at a time with hand grenades, explosives, and flamethrowers.

From Yalta to Berlin

In early February 1945, as the Allied armies closed in on the German heartland—the British and Americans from the west, the Soviets from the east—their political leaders met to plan the war's end and aftermath.

For what would be their final meeting, Roosevelt, Churchill, and Stalin came together at Yalta in the Russian Crimea amid the ravages of the recent German occupation. In the week-long conference, they coordinated their final offensives against the Third Reich and decided upon zones for the postwar occupation. Roosevelt obtained Stalin's commitment to enter the war against Japan within a few months after the German capitulation. He also persuaded Stalin to agree to participate in the proposed United Nations by offering a voting formula under which the major powers would have a veto. Stalin in return was to be allowed a free hand in Eastern Europe, except in Poland where he pledged an independent government. He broke this promise within weeks.

One indirect consequence of Yalta was the indiscriminate bombing of Dresden, a beautiful old city without vital military targets. Roosevelt and Churchill wanted to cultivate Stalin by bombing cities in eastern Germany, ostensibly to aid the Soviet advance. On the night of February 13, two days after the conference ended, nearly 800 British bombers dropped almost 3,000 tons of bombs on Dresden—about half of them incendiaries. They created a firestorm that generated winds of tornado force, incinerated everything in its path, and even sucked the life out of those taking shelter in cellars. About 10 hours later, more than 300 American bombers arrived to deliver additional devastation: nearly 800 tons of high explosives targeted on railroad facilities.

The city was practically leveled to the ground (*right*). Initial estimates of the death toll ranged as high as 250,000. Though this was later revised sharply downward to 35,000, Dresden became for many an enduring symbol of air power run amok.

Into the Heartland. While the bombers were at work, British and American ground troops had broken free of the Ardennes, where they had been bottled up by the Battle of the Bulge. They fought their way through the Siegfried

Gathering at Yalta in the Russian Crimea for their last conference, the leaders of the Big Three powers pose for a formal portrait. Roosevelt's worn and weary face reflected his failing health—a factor that may have helped give Stalin the upper hand in their dealings.

A sandstone statue atop Dresden's town hall appears to reach out toward the ruins of the old city. Consecutive British and U.S. bombing raids on February 13 and 14 set off devastating fires that burned for a week.

En route to the Rhine in late February, GIs cross a footbridge strung by army engineers over the Rur River. The dead soldier was hit by mortar fragments just 50 feet short of the east bank.

Crossing the Rhine at Oppenheim in late March, Third Army soldiers hunch down in their assault boats to elude fire from Germans on the east bank. The following day, their commander, General George Patton, strode halfway across a newly erected pontoon bridge and urinated in the middle of the river as a gesture of contempt for the enemy.

Line of fortifications along the German border, moving relentlessly toward the Rhine River. "The more Germans we kill west of the Rhine," Eisenhower said, "the fewer there will be to meet us east of the river." The Rhine was the last formidable barrier in western Germany. Coursing from Switzerland to the North Sea, it was 550 yards wide in places, its turbulent waters flanked by cliffs and high hills that severely limited available crossing points.

The Germans retreating across the Rhine blew up every bridge but one. This was the railroad span at Remagen, a small town roughly in the center of the front.

When Company A of the Ninth Armored Division rode into town on March 7, members were astonished to find the bridge still standing. They watched German engineers twice attempt to detonate the bridge and fail both times. Then, following the shouted orders of their company commander, they sprinted across the span.

Other bridgeheads followed. Two weeks later, to the south at Oppenheim, Patton's Third Army sneaked across the river at night in assault boats to preempt the long-scheduled crossing in the north of his hated rival, British field marshal Bernard Montgomery. Near the Dutch border,

> "I pray you to believe what I have said about Buchenwald. I have reported what I saw and heard, but only part of it. For most of it I have no words."
>
> Edward R. Murrow, April 1945

At Buchenwald (left), residents from the nearby city of Weimar walk with eyes averted past piled-up corpses; Patton had summoned the civilians to witness evidence of Nazi atrocities. At right, survivors pose for the camera of Life magazine's Margaret Bourke-White, one of the first journalists to reach Buchenwald.

Montgomery's forces crossed a day later after an aerial and artillery bombardment that lit up the sky for 40 miles.

By the beginning of April, the Allies had six bridgeheads across the Rhine on a 200-mile front. The U.S. First and Ninth Armies moved out to encircle the Ruhr Valley, Germany's mining and industrial center, and captured 325,000 troops in the war's largest mass surrender. Other armies sped eastward.

As they advanced, the Allies came face to face with the horrors of Nazi brutality. The Soviets already had reported uncovering in Poland the remains of Auschwitz and other German extermination camps responsible for the gassing deaths of millions of Jews. These reports had met with some skepticism in the West. But in April, the British and Americans began liberating concentration camps, where the Germans had imprisoned not only Jews but Russian and Polish prisoners of war, Gypsies, homosexuals, criminals, and Communists and other political dissidents. These

were the Reich's slave laborers for whom death came more slowly than in the eastern extermination camps—through overwork, malnutrition, disease, and random executions.

The first western camp liberated was at Ohrdruf, one of 136 satellites of the huge Buchenwald complex in central Germany. Eisenhower, Bradley, and Patton visited Ohrdruf less than a week after its liberation and were stunned at the sight of unburied corpses and emaciated prisoners on the brink of death. Bradley was speechless. The gruff Patton vomited. Eisenhower, experiencing a powerful urge "to testify at first-hand about these things," sent cables to London and Washington urging journalists and legislators to come see for themselves. He wanted the evidence "immediately placed before the American and British publics in a fashion that would leave no room for cynical doubt." Because of Ike's concern, when Buchenwald itself was liberated a few days later, journalists such as Edward R. Murrow of CBS Radio and photographer Mar-

garet Bourke-White of *Life* were there to record the truth.

On April 12, the same day that Ike visited the Ohrdruf camp, he lost his commander in chief. Only 63 years old but prematurely aged after more than 12 years in office, Roosevelt was at his vacation retreat in Warm Springs, Georgia, enjoying a beautiful morning. An artist was painting his portrait. After awhile, Roosevelt raised his hand to the back of his neck and said quietly, "I have a terrific pain in the back of my head." Then he slumped over. Two and a half hours later, he was dead of a cerebral hemorrhage. The nation—and indeed many people throughout the world—went into mourning. Appropriately, his

death appeared in the regular army-navy lists of war casualties: "Roosevelt, Franklin D., Commander in Chief."

The Final Days. On the day FDR died, fast-moving U.S. tanks drove to within a hard day's march of Berlin. Churchill wanted Eisenhower to push on and get there before the Soviets, who were regrouping 35 miles east of Berlin, where they faced the bulk of the remaining German army. But Eisenhower knew that under the Yalta agreements the Soviet postwar occupation zone would include Berlin and extend from there 60 miles westward to the Elbe River. He estimated the capture of Berlin would cost him

Freckle-Faced Hero

Congressional Medal of Honor

Distinguished Service Cross

Legion of Merit

Farmersville, Texas—population 2,206—turned out en masse on June 15, 1945, to welcome home Lieutenant Audie Murphy, back from the battlefields of North Africa, Italy, and France. Six months earlier, Audie had saved his entire company from a surprise attack by six tanks and 250 German infantrymen. This heroic act won him the Congressional Medal of Honor (which he wears at left), with the citation quoted below. It was one of some 25 awards this orphaned son of sharecroppers earned, making him at 21 America's most decorated soldier of the war.

Tongues wagged when Audie gave his medals to children, but he said, "I didn't feel that they entirely belonged to me. My whole unit earned them, but I didn't know how to give them to the whole unit."

". . . Lieutenant Murphy climbed on the burning tank destroyer, which was in danger of blowing up at any moment, and employed its .50 caliber machine gun against the enemy. He was alone and exposed to German fire from three sides, but his deadly fire killed dozens of Germans and caused their infantry attack to waver."

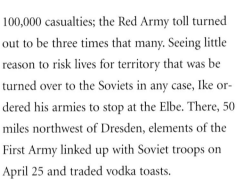

100,000 casualties; the Red Army toll turned out to be three times that many. Seeing little reason to risk lives for territory that was be turned over to the Soviets in any case, Ike ordered his armies to stop at the Elbe. There, 50 miles northwest of Dresden, elements of the First Army linked up with Soviet troops on April 25 and traded vodka toasts.

In Berlin, meanwhile, Hitler was holed up in his underground bunker. On April 30, he could hear the shells exploding above his 19-room compound. The Soviets, fighting block by block against fanatical last-ditch German resistance, were only a few hundred yards away. Hitler was determined to avoid the fate of his old Italian ally Mussolini, who had been shot by partisans two days before, then strung up by his heels. That afternoon, he administered a cyanide capsule to his new bride, Eva Braun, and then shot himself in the mouth. He was 56 years old.

A week later, at the little red schoolhouse that served as Eisenhower's headquarters in the French town of Reims, General Alfred Gustav Jodl, chief of staff of what remained of the German army, agreed to an unconditional surrender. Eisenhower relayed the momentous news to his superiors in London and Washington with the most succinct of messages: "The mission of this Allied force was fulfilled at 0241 local time, May 7, 1945."

On the long final journey from Georgia to the ancestral home in Hyde Park, New York, the caisson bearing the flag-draped coffin of President Roosevelt passes in front of the White House. Vice President Harry S Truman felt woefully ill prepared to succeed Roosevelt. "The whole weight of the moon and stars fell on me," he told reporters. "Please pray for me."

Hours before the official proclamation of victory in Europe on May 8, an estimated 500,000 New Yorkers celebrate in Times Square around a replica of the Statue of Liberty. Because the Soviets insisted on a delay while they repeated the surrender ritual in Berlin, V-E Day was not observed in the U.S.S.R. until May 9.

Black smoke billows from the carrier Bunker Hill after two kamikaze planes crashed into its flight deck near Okinawa. The two explosions, 30 seconds apart, ignited a deck full of aircraft loaded with bombs and gasoline. Almost 400 men died.

Fiery Stand at Japan's Doorstep

Okinawa, the last island steppingstone to Japan, offered the same familiar enemy fanaticism, but more desperately applied. The Japanese prepared to defend this island less than 350 miles from their homeland with the most massive attacks of kamikaze suicide planes so far, aimed at turning U.S. ships into raging infernos.

On April 1, in the largest amphibious operation of the Pacific war, a U.S. armada of 1,300 vessels landed 60,000 troops on the western coast of Okinawa. Meeting little resistance, they soon controlled most of the northern two-thirds of the island. But in the south, the bulk of the enemy's 120,000 defenders were so well entrenched that the invaders would have to pay dearly for every inch.

While ground troops engaged in grueling combat, the Japanese mounted a series of 10 mass kamikaze attacks against the U.S. ships

> "We watched each plunging kamikaze with the detached horror of one witnessing a terrible spectacle rather than as the intended victim."
>
> American naval officer

standing offshore. The first of these onslaughts, known as *kikusui* ("floating chrysanthemums"), occurred on April 6 and involved 355 aircraft. Before taking off on their fatal missions from Kyushu, the southernmost Japanese island, the pilots were feted at banquets, entertained by geishas, and praised as modern samurai warriors.

Despite the sacrifice of some 1,900 kamikaze pilots, the two-month-long kikusui campaign failed in its goal of driving off the U.S. fleet and leaving the invaders trapped helplessly on Okinawa. But the U.S. Navy suffered its worst losses of the war with 29 ships sunk, 368 others damaged, and 5,000 men killed. Another kind of suicide mission proved less

> ## "We were all psychotic, inmates of the greatest madhouse in history, but staying on the line was a matter of pride."

U.S. Marine Sergeant William Manchester

destructive. The Japanese dispatched the showpiece of their crippled navy, the battleship *Yamato*, with sufficient fuel to reach Okinawa but not enough to return home. A swarm of U.S. air attacks sent the *Yamato* and five of its escort ships to the bottom before they could do any harm.

On southern Okinawa, meanwhile, the fighting focused on dislodging the Japanese from a series of hills and ridges that the Americans dubbed with innocuous names such as Sugar Loaf and Chocolate Drop. The GIs employed tactics that the 10th Army commander, Lieutenant General Simon Buckner, called "blowtorch and corkscrew": Blast the dugout entrance with flamethrowers and then seal it with grenades or explosives.

The island was finally secured on June 22. It had taken the Americans almost three months and a death toll of more than 7,000 men—including General Buckner, whose heart was pierced by a flying rock fragment chipped off by an artillery shell. Among the 110,000 dead Japanese defenders was their able commander, Lieutenant General Missuru Ushijima, who donned his medals, knelt on a ceremonial quilt, and committed hara-kiri.

The invasion of Japan was next on the United States agenda. Some planners feared it might cost up to one million American casualties.

Wounded in the head and foot, his hands clasped as if in prayer, a GI from the Seventh Infantry Division awaits evacuation at the base of the enemy strongpoints on southern Okinawa known as Rocky Crags.

The Soldiers' Storyteller

The GIs' favorite war correspondent was skinny, gray-haired Ernie Pyle, who had shared with them the front-line hazards of North Africa, Sicily, and Italy. So closely did he identify with the common soldier—whose loneliness and fears he covered better than anyone—that Pyle felt duty bound to report from the Pacific as well. In January 1945, the 44-year-old Pulitzer Prize winner shipped out. From Okinawa he wrote to his wife, "I've promised myself and I promise you that if I come through this one I will never go on another one." Three weeks later, on the tiny island of Ie Shima, just west of Okinawa, Pyle was killed by a sniper's bullet. GIs erected a marker that read, "On this spot the 77th Infantry Division lost a buddy, Ernie Pyle."

Robert Oppenheimer (left) and General Leslie Groves inspect the site of the first atomic test in New Mexico. The tangle of steel was all that remained of the test tower, which endured heat four times the core temperature of the sun.

"The Destroyer of Worlds"

For months, B-29 Superfortresses had rained fire upon the Japanese home islands. Adopting the incendiary raids pioneered by the British against Germany, they burned out more than half the total area of Japan's 66 largest cities. One raid against Tokyo created such an immense firestorm that 16 square miles were consumed and 100,000 people were killed.

But a far more fearsome weapon awaited. Its origins dated back to a letter to President Roosevelt written by Albert Einstein in 1939. If its atoms were split, the physicist suggested, "the element uranium may be turned into a new and important source of energy." Harnessing this energy in a bomb became the focus of the $2 billion Manhattan Project—so named because the initial research took place at Columbia University, in Manhattan. In 1942, on a squash court under the unused football sta-

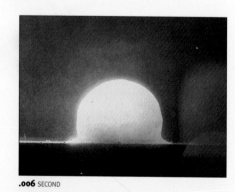

.006 SECOND

.016 SECOND

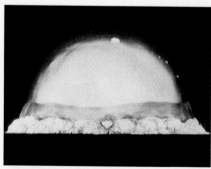

.034 SECOND

2 SECONDS

4 SECONDS

6 SECONDS

dium at the University of Chicago, a team led by the Italian exile Enrico Fermi achieved the first controlled nuclear chain reaction. Then, at newly built complexes at Oak Ridge, Tennessee, and Hanford, Washington, thousands of workers began producing the rare materials needed. The work proceeded in such secrecy that Harry Truman did not even know about it until the day after he was sworn in as president.

The task of making and testing the bomb was assigned to a new laboratory in the mountains at Los Alamos, New Mexico. The brainpower gathered there was so eccentrically brilliant that General Leslie Groves, the abrasive but effective chief of the Manhattan Project, referred to the scientists as "the largest collection of crackpots ever seen."

The first test took place on July 16, 1945. At a site in the desert the Spanish had called Jornada del Muerto—"Journey of Death"—an atomic bomb suspended from a 100-foot-high steel tower was detonated by remote control. The blast, equal to 17,000 tons of TNT, was so bright that bewildered New Mexicans thought the sun had risen twice that day. A darker thought, a passage from a sacred Hindu text, occurred to the project's scientific director, J. Robert Oppenheimer: "I am

The explosive dawn of the atomic age is documented in the timed sequence below, which captures the first 15 seconds of the New Mexico test on July 16, 1945. Images in the top row, taken with a telephoto lens during the first second after detonation, reveal boiling debris and gaseous flame bursting forth. Subsequent images in the bottom row, shot with a normal lens, show the emergence of the towering mushroom-shaped cloud that would become the symbol of the nuclear era.

.072 SECOND

.1 SECOND

1 SECOND

8 SECONDS

10 SECONDS

15 SECONDS

A mushroom-shaped pillar of radioactive steam, dust, and ash towers over Nagasaki, site of the second atomic attack against Japan. The lethal cloud rose more than 12 miles above the stricken city.

become Death, the destroyer of worlds."

News of the success reached President Truman at the Big Three conference at Potsdam near Berlin. He told Stalin that the United States "had a new weapon of unusual destructive force." Stalin showed little interest—he already knew about the atomic bomb through a Soviet spy at Los Alamos—but simply said he hoped the U.S. would make "good use of it against the Japanese." Truman did not hesitate. Hoping to avoid an invasion and end the war in one stroke, he gave the go-ahead.

At 8:15 a.m. on August 6, a B-29 named Enola Gay after the mother of the pilot, Colonel Paul Tibbets Jr., released an atomic bomb over the city of Hiroshima. The bomb, a uranium device nicknamed Little Boy, exploded with such force that people standing near ground zero had their shadows burned into the concrete. Four square miles of the city were erased. Nearly 100,000 people were killed that day. Perhaps twice as many more would die later from burns and the effects of radiation.

When the Japanese failed to respond to Truman's warning of "a rain of ruin," he ordered a second attack. On August 9, "Fat Man," a plutonium bomb, fell on Nagasaki. Though it packed more power than the uranium version, steep hills in and around the city contained the blast, limiting damage and the immediate death toll to 35,000. The United States nuclear arsenal was now temporarily depleted, but Little Boy and Fat Man had done their terrible work.

Awaiting treatment on the morning after the bomb was dropped on Nagasaki, a victim sips water from a canteen. She and the others in this photograph died before help arrived. Among those exposed to the atomic blasts, the dying did not stop for many years to come.

"They may expect a rain of ruin from the air, the like of which has never been seen on this earth."

President Truman, August 7, 1945

Peace at Last on a Day for Kisses

Emperor Hirohito had had enough. Throughout the war he had passively acquiesced in both his nation's aggression and its devastation. But on August 9, the United States had obliterated Nagasaki and the Russians had finally come into the war against Japan, invading the puppet state in Manchuria. That night, in the imperial bomb shelter, Hirohito took an extraordinary step. He intervened in the deliberations of his Supreme War Council, which had deadlocked over the issue of whether to go on fighting to the death. "The time has come," he said, "when we must bear the unbearable."

The U.S. agreed to the new Japanese offer of unconditional surrender with the emperor remaining on his throne. President Truman made the announcement on August 14. All around the world, on what one GI called "the kissingest day in history," people celebrated V-J Day and the arrival of peace. The following day, astonished Japanese heard their emperor utter his first words in pub-

In Paris (left), U.S. servicemen and women display the day's news. In Times Square (above), a sailor celebrates with army nurse Edith Shain.

lic. In a radio broadcast to his 100 million subjects, he managed to announce Japan's capitulation without ever using the words "surrender" or "defeat."

Formal surrender awaited the arrival in Tokyo Bay of the battleship fittingly named for the president's home state. On the quarterdeck of the *Missouri,* on Sunday, September 2, representatives of the combatants signed the necessary papers. General MacArthur, casual in an open-necked uniform shirt without tie or decorations, spoke in the spirit of reconciliation that would mark his postwar tenure as governor of occupied Japan. "It is my earnest hope," he said, "that from this solemn occasion a better world shall emerge out of the blood and carnage of the past."

The greatest war the world had ever known was over.

The Cost of War

Military Deaths	
Total Allied deaths	**14,201,000**
United States	274,000
United Kingdom	300,000
France	250,000
China	2,500,000
Soviet Union	10,000,000
Total Axis deaths	**7,674,000**
Germany	4,500,000
Japan	2,000,000
Civilian Deaths	
Total Allied deaths	**24,042,000**
United States	—
United Kingdom	50,000
France	350,000
China	7,400,000
Soviet Union	10,000,000
Total Axis deaths	**3,080,000**
Germany	2,000,000
Japan	350,000
Concentration camp deaths	**12,000,000**

Aboard the battleship Missouri, representatives of the Allies and Japan face each other across a table on September 2. General Yoshiro Umezu signs the surrender while MacArthur (far right) watches.

Beloved heavyweight champion Joe Louis performs in a wartime exhibition. Louis was awarded the Legion of Merit in September 1945 for entertaining fellow servicemen in dozens of such events throughout the war.

A radiant Bess Myerson poses in full Miss America regalia. She was the first college graduate to wear the crown.

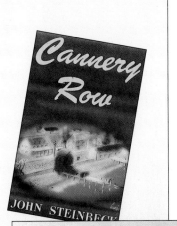

★ 1945

Arts and Entertainment

"I never hated any man," observed boxing champion Joe Louis, "not even in the ring." Louis had earned the heavyweight title in 1937 and held on to it for 12 years. He enlisted in the army in January 1942, inspiring both blacks and whites with his patriotism and calm advocacy of racial equality. Bess Myerson, the first Jewish Miss America, also used her title to speak out against racial intolerance.

Revolutions of a different sort were taking place in the performing arts. Martha Graham *(below, right)*, considered by some to be the Picasso of dance, used physical tension and abstracted gestures to explore themes of art, mythology, and the human psyche— and in the process give dance a whole new look and mood.

John Steinbeck's Cannery Row and Paramount Pictures' Lost Weekend shunned idealized visions of society to examine human failings.

Martha Graham's jubilant modern dance Appalachian Spring, with music by Aaron Copland, had its Washington debut on October 30, 1945. The work celebrated the American pioneer spirit.

Home Sweet Home

★

BACK IN THE USA

After Japan's surrender, spontaneous celebrations swept the nation—from Times Square, where more than a million people crowded together to cheer the war's end, to the village of Barrow, Alaska, where a dozen Inuits broke into a dance to the beat of walrus-skin drums. But when the initial outbursts of joy subsided, there was only one thing on people's minds: getting the troops back home. Thousands of families flooded Washington with pleas to have their loved ones returned to them right away. One senator received 200 pairs of baby booties with "I miss my daddy!" tags attached. President Truman moved quickly to demobilize the troops, even using British ships such as the *Queen Mary (right)* to transport servicemen back to the States.

Although they were often downright silly with joy at being home *(left)*, many GIs found adjustment to postwar life difficult. The wartime economy was shifting to a peacetime one; jobs and houses were scarce at first, and the prices of consumer goods soared. But by 1947 an economic boom had started, and with it came a boom of another kind—in babies. Soon Americans were buying up a host of newfangled goods, from washing machines *(pages 170-171)* to the latest source of home entertainment— the television. As one magazine put it, the blackout days were over: "This is the dream era."

Home from the war, an elated airman kisses American soil. When the fighting finally ended in the Pacific, there were still some seven million troops overseas.

1946-1949

★

Life Goes On

For the millions of servicemen returning in the first months after the war, the army magazine *Yank* said it all as it jokingly introduced them to their new "uniform": the business suit *(inset)*. Indeed, most of them did shed military clothes for a suit or a pair of workingman's overalls. They saw in postwar America a chance to don a new and better life for themselves and their families. As one veteran put it: "The guys who came out of World War II were idealistic. They sincerely believed that this time they were coming home to build a new world."

The dream got a rough start. As part of the guns-to-butter economic transition, many factories and other businesses had to lay off workers. Women were especially hard hit by the layoffs; in 1947, pink slips were handed out to almost two million working women. Within months, factories had retooled and began churning out consumer goods at a record pace, but almost all the new jobs went to men. Inflation added to the turmoil. After Congress lifted wartime price and wage controls in 1946, the cost of almost everything, from shoes to shaving cream, shot up dramatically—often by more than 100 percent. "Prices Soar, Buyers Sore," noted a New York

Unemployed GIs, like these hanging out in a soda shop, were known as members of the 52-20 Club because they could receive unemployment pay of $20 for 52 weeks under the GI Bill. Most veterans, however, remained in the "club" for an average of only four months.

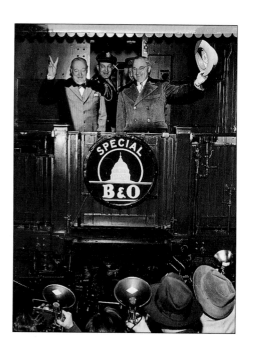

"An iron curtain has descended across the Continent."

Winston Churchill, March 5, 1946

Winston Churchill displays his well-known victory sign while standing next to President Truman during a 1946 tour of the United States. At one stop on the tour, Churchill gave his famous "Iron Curtain" speech, in which he called on Americans to join Britons in opposing Soviet expansion in Eastern Europe.

U.S. Marines arrive in the Japanese port city of Saga in 1946 as part of the Allied occupational forces. Within a year, Japan had a new democratic constitution that included a pledge to never again amass military forces.

Daily News headline. And wages failed to keep pace with the skyrocketing cost of living, much to the anger of labor unions, who staged loud and frequent strikes.

The GI Bill. Anticipating that returning veterans might be especially prone to economic problems, in 1944 Congress had passed the Servicemen's Readjustment Act, soon dubbed the GI Bill of Rights. This landmark legislation offered veterans a year of unemployment benefits, money for college education or job training, and low-interest loans to buy a home, farm, or business.

Few of the men returning from Europe and Asia had earned even a high-school diploma before the war. Now millions of them took advantage of the $500 yearly tuition plus monthly living allowance of the GI Bill and crammed into college and technical school classrooms across the country. In 1949, the nation's colleges turned out twice as many graduates as a decade earlier. Almost overnight, the GI Bill created a large, educated middle class with significant disposable income, giving the whole economy a boost.

A New Threat. Even as America straightened up its domestic affairs, it worked to put the world's house in order as well—a task made all the more urgent by a new global threat. In Eastern Europe, the U.S.'s wartime ally the Soviet Union had become the enemy, spreading Communism and its own brand of tyranny to country after country; China, too, would go Communist under Mao Zedong. By 1947, President Truman decided that Communism had to be contained in Europe and sent money to Turkey and Greece to keep their governments from falling to the Communists. Aid was also sent to Japan, which was occupied by the Allied forces under the leadership of General Douglas MacArthur. After demilitarizing the country, MacArthur directed Japan's postwar government to create a new, democratic constitution, which served as a further bulwark against both Communism and any possible militaristic revival.

Near decade's end, the United States and 11 other countries would form the North Atlantic Treaty Organization (NATO) as a deterrent to Communist aggression. But the threat was already there, even if not in the form of direct military action. As American financier Bernard Baruch put it in April 1947: "Let us not be deceived—today we are in the midst of a cold war."

Nazis on Trial

The magnitude of the atrocities perpetrated by Nazi leaders during the war resulted in one of the most compelling trials ever. A total of 22 high-ranking officers, including Hermann Göring (above)—the number one Nazi after Hitler—stood accused of "crimes against humanity," including mass exterminations and genocide. Civilization itself, said U.S. prosecutor Robert H. Jackson, "was the real complaining party."

Held in Nuremberg, scene of the Nazis' annual rallies, the trial took 216 days. Witness testimony, photographs, and newsreels all documented the horror: the slave labor, the torture, the sadistic medical experiments, and the gassing and murder of 11 million Jews, prisoners of war, and other captives. On October 1, 1946, the four Allied judges found 19 of the 22 guilty, and sentenced 12—including Göring—to death by hanging.

Suburbia Rampant

With a thriving economy and easy government credit for education and mortgages, couples began flocking to the altar after the war. In 1946 more than 2.2 million couples, twice as many as in any previous year, exchanged vows. That record would stand for 33 years. Not surprisingly, the next year saw another record: the birth of 3.8 million babies. By decade's end, American women had delivered some 32 million babies—8 million more than during the previous decade.

Right after the war, housing was scarce, and newlyweds often had to move in with friends or relatives. Then a New York businessman named William J. Levitt had a brainstorm: Why not build houses like cars, using assembly-line techniques? Within months he began constructing a prefabricated housing development on 6,000 acres of Long Island potato fields. The look-alike houses were small but inexpensive, some costing less than $8,000. All were equipped with modern appliances and surrounded by shops and parks.

Levittown, as the new community was called, was an instant success. The homes sold quickly—even before they were built—and people camped out for days in the hope of getting a chance to buy one. Soon other builders were erecting similar developments on the outskirts of cities around the country. The great postwar migration from the cities to the suburbs had begun.

Rows of nearly identical newly built houses line the streets of Lakewood, California, in 1949. Although some social critics decried the drab uniformity of such developments, they were wildly popular.

"I called the builder up and said I'll buy one and he said don't you want to look at it and I said no."

Veteran Karl Hayman

A sponsored participant (left) takes off at a crawl in pursuit of stuffed-animal prizes during a "Diaper Derby" in Palisades Park, New Jersey. As the marriage and birth rates soared, moms, strollers, and toddlers became common sights in Levittown, New York (right), and other new suburbs across the country.

MILLIONS OF WOMEN HAVE THEIR HEARTS SET ON A NEW *Maytag*

Pitching the New Prosperity

Dreams came true for eager consumers in the world of postwar advertisements as companies went after the new flow of dollars. Detroit emphasized trend-setting in automobile design *(bottom)*, while Westinghouse offered a cornucopia of appliances to plug in and turn on *(right)*.

New Popular-Priced Hoover

THE HOOVER

TRAIL BLAZERS
IN POSTWAR STYLING!

Home Freezer · Refrigerator · Ironer · Laundromatt · Clothes Dryer · Radio · Water Heater · Vacuum Cleaners · Fan · Automatic Iron · Toaster · Roaster Oven · Sandwich Grill · Waffle Baker · Room Heater · Hot Plate · Percolator · Coffee Maker · Warming Pad · Air Conditioner · Washer · Dishwasher · Range

B-7-46 REFRIGERATOR
$179.95
...including Federal Excise Tax, a 5-year protection plan and delivery to your home.

Every house needs Westinghouse

Maker of 30 MILLION Electric Home Appliances

WESTINGHOUSE ELECTRIC CORPORATION · PLANTS IN 25 CITIES · OFFICES EVERYWHERE · APPLIANCE DIVISION, MANSFIELD, OHIO

Tune In: John Charles Thomas, Sun. 2:30 EST., N.B.C. · Ted Malone, Mon. Through Fri., 11:45 A.M., EST., American Broadcasting Co. Network

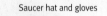

Saucer hat and gloves

"Global" derby with veil

Striped John-Frederics hat

Fancy sunglasses for the beach

Fluted "abbess" bonnet

French two-piece swimsuit
with hairband

Simple cloche

Fashion Takes Off

The trim, spartan suits and ruffle-less blouses of women's fashion during the war years—when fabric was at a premium—gave way to unbridled luxury by the late 1940s. French designer Christian Dior led the trend with his high-fashion "New Look," employing full skirts, narrow waists, and padded hips and busts to accentuate feminine curves. Many American women rejoiced in their freedom from no-frills wartime austerity by wearing inexpensive copies of Dior originals.

Accessories for these opulent styles often ran to the bizarre, especially when it came to hats. Some of the most exotic headpieces could cost more than dress, shoes, and other accouterments combined. "Let's try something new!" seemed to be the prevailing wisdom, one that by the end of the decade helped introduce a fashion mainstay—the bikini.

Spike-heeled sandal with ankle strap

Models pose in haute couture outfits in 1947. A shapely silhouette and abundant fabric defined the postwar look.

The Red Scare Hits Home

Just one month after the end of the war, Americans got a jolt when a defecting Soviet official revealed evidence of extensive Soviet espionage throughout North America. Frightened and angered by the idea that Communist spies could be living among them, citizens reacted in both reasonable and unreasonable ways, and the government followed suit. Soon full-blown Red hysteria was sweeping the nation.

By 1947 many government officials, college professors, and others were required to sign "loyalty oaths"—declarations that they were loyal Americans and had no Communist sympathies. People who refused to sign, including 120 professors at the University of California-Los Angeles, often lost their jobs.

In Congress, the House Un-American Activities Committee held hearings in 1947 to determine whether "Communist propaganda" was making its way into movies. The committee called dozens of witnesses, including producer Walt Disney and actor Ronald Reagan. Some witnesses—those deemed "unfriendly"—were asked point-blank: "Are you now or have you ever been a member of the Communist Party?" Ten people, including writer Ring Lardner Jr., claimed the question violated their First Amendment rights and refused to answer. The committee sent them off to jail for contempt of Congress.

The committee's next round of hearings focused on the State Department. Whittaker Chambers, a *Time* magazine editor, accused former State Department official Alger Hiss of being a Communist agent. Hiss denied the charge under oath. Chambers then produced evidence, including several rolls of microfilm, which he dramatically pulled out of their hiding place—a pumpkin on his Maryland farm. Hiss, still maintaining his innocence, was convicted of perjury and sent to prison.

Several Republican members of the House Un-American Activities Committee, including Congressman Richard Nixon (far right), pose for a photograph in 1948. The committee's chairman, J. Parnell Thomas (second from left), went to prison several years later for illegally padding his congressional office's payroll.

" Party labels don't mean anything anymore. You can draw a line right down the middle. On one side are the Americans; on the other are the Communists and Socialists."

Actor George Murphy

Some of Hollywood's best-known actors, including Lauren Bacall, Humphrey Bogart, Danny Kaye, and Gene Kelly, deplane in Washington on their way to protest the investigations of the House Un-American Activities Committee. Communist hysteria led to the blacklisting of hundreds of writers, directors, and actors.

Jackie Robinson slides hard into third base during his history-making rookie year in the major leagues. Two years later, in 1949, his aggressive style and all-around excellent play earned him baseball's top individual honor in the National League, the Most Valuable Player award.

Breaking Baseball's Color Barrier

Power hitter Larry Doby (above) signed with Cleveland three months after Robinson's debut, becoming the American League's first black player. Pitcher Satchel Paige (below) joined the team in 1948.

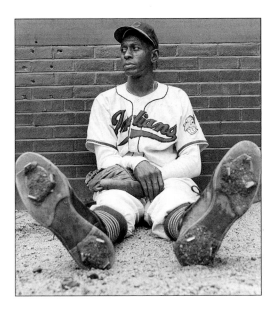

He was arguably one of baseball's best pitchers, a veteran of the Negro leagues for some 20 years. But Leroy "Satchel" Paige *(left, below)*—along with every other black player in the game—was not allowed to play in the major leagues for one simple reason: the color of his skin. In the fall of 1945, Branch Rickey—president of the National League's Brooklyn Dodgers—decided it was time to renounce this shameful legacy. Against the objections of almost everyone else in baseball, he signed 28-year-old Jackie Robinson *(opposite)* to the Dodgers AAA farm club, the Montreal Royals. Rickey warned Robinson that he would have to find the courage not to respond to racial taunts on or off the field—or risk setting off a race riot that might keep baseball segregated for another 20 years.

Robinson said he was ready for the challenge—and he clearly was. Despite relentless abuse that ranged from intentional cleatings by fellow players to death threats, Robinson, showing iron self-control, never retaliated. Instead, he concentrated on playing good ball. In 1947, after only one year with the Royals, Robinson was brought up to play for the Dodgers. He proceeded to help lead them to the pennant, and won the very first Rookie of the Year award. The barrier was broken, and soon more black players joined Robinson—including, at last, the great Satchel.

"Twenty-two years is a long time to be a rookie."

Satchel Paige

American Aid to Rescue Europe

The Cold War did nothing but heat up as the U.S.S.R. continued to expand its influence in Eastern Europe. And again, America responded with an infusion of aid to bolster Europe's democracies. After Communists staged a coup in Czechoslovakia in 1948, Congress approved the Marshall Plan, a huge economic aid package for Europe developed by Truman's secretary of state, George C. Marshall *(left)*. Its effect was dramatic. Impoverished people throughout Europe received food, clothing, and other desperately needed goods. Railroads and factories were rebuilt; mines became productive again. For much of Western Europe, economic health had been restored.

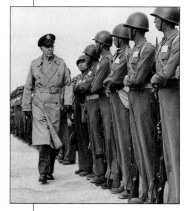

But tensions between the United States and the Soviet Union continued to mount. A major crisis developed later in 1948 over the fate of West Berlin, the non-Soviet sector of the divided city that lay 110 miles inside Soviet-controlled East Germany. When the Soviets blockaded all land routes to the city, the United States and Britain responded by airlifting food and supplies in, around the clock, for 321 days. The Soviets finally lifted the blockade in May 1949. Western nations had won their first major Cold War victory. There was little chance to celebrate: Four months later, the Soviet Union detonated its first nuclear bomb, throwing a dark and ever lengthening shadow over hopes for a lasting world peace.

General George Marshall inspects troops in China, where he briefly served as U.S. ambassador (inset). His economic recovery plan for Europe won him the Nobel Peace Prize in 1953.

An Austrian boy hugs a new pair of shoes given to him by Red Cross volunteers. The United States' $13 billion Marshall Plan made such donations possible. A London newspaper called the aid "the most . . . generous thing that any country has ever done for others."

An American C-47, loaded with tons of dehydrated potatoes and meat, approaches West Berlin's Tempelhof Field during the Berlin Airlift. Hundreds of British and American planes landed daily at the city's two airfields—at a rate of up to one every four minutes.

"Give 'em Hell" Harry Wins

According to the polls, President Harry Truman had little chance of winning the 1948 presidential election. Many voters, it seemed, blamed him for the country's postwar problems. "To err is Truman," people joked. One newspaper even suggested he concede to his Republican opponent, Governor Thomas Dewey of New York, and save the nation "the wear and tear of campaigning."

Truman was not about to give up. He boarded a train for a whistle-stop tour of the country, talking to farmers and city folk alike about his plans and positions and berating the "do nothing" Republican-led Congress. Crowds often responded by shouting, "Give 'em hell, Harry!"

Early on election night, Dewey declared victory. At 9:00 p.m., Truman took a bath, ate a small dinner, and went to bed. He awoke several hours later to learn that he had pulled off one of the biggest political upsets in American history: He had won the election by more than two million votes.

"I never gave anybody hell. I just told the truth and they thought it was hell."

Harry Truman

After his stunning election upset, an exuberant Harry Truman holds up an early edition of the Chicago Daily Tribune, which erroneously announced his defeat.

Comedian Bob Hope (left) and singer Bing Crosby (right) clown their way through a musical number from their film Road to Utopia.

★ **1946 - 1949**

Arts and Entertainment

Uplifting movies like 1947's *It's a Wonderful Life (poster, above)* and escapist fare such as Hope-Crosby comedies and Humphrey Bogart tough-guy dramas were hugely popular in the late 1940s. On Broadway, postwar America saw the debut of two of its greatest playwrights, Tennessee Williams and Arthur Miller. Musicals were still big hits too, and the songwriting team of Richard Rodgers and Oscar Hammerstein added another success with *South Pacific* in 1949.

Offstage, a new form of entertainment was gaining momentum: television. The three broadcast networks expanded their programming, offering news, sports, and variety shows, all in black and white. By the end of the decade there were nearly 10 million TV sets in American homes.

Marlon Brando as Stanley Kowalski kneels before his wife, Stella (Kim Hunter), in the 1947 Broadway production of Tennessee Williams's A Streetcar Named Desire.

The Howdy Doody Show

Premiering in late 1947, Buffalo Bob and his marionette, Howdy Doody, won raves from adults and kids alike.

Texaco Star Theater

TV's first big star, Milton Berle, began hosting his enormously popular variety show in 1948.

*Fred Astaire levitates during the number "Puttin'
on the Ritz" from the movie musical Blue Skies.
His matchless grace epitomized 1940s high style.*

Mary Martin skips across stage in South Pacific. Lighthearted but with a dark edge, the show recalled the sorrows and hopes of a bittersweet time.

ACKNOWLEDGMENTS

The editors wish to thank the following individuals and institutions for their valuable assistance in the preparation of this volume:
Richard Allen, Lynden, Wash.; Judy and Ed Ashley, Jed Collectibles, Pemberton, N.J.; Bob Brewer, Los Alamos National Laboratory, Los Alamos, N.Mex.; Stan Cohen, Pictorial Histories Publishing Company, Missoula, Mont.; Tom Conroy, Movie Still Archives, Harrison, Nebr.; Cyndy Gilley, Do You Graphics, Woodbine, Md.; Scott Gruber, United Services Organization, Washington, D.C.; Mary Ison and staff, Library of Congress, Washington, D.C.; Marine Corps Historical Center, Washington, D.C.; Jack Matthews, Kiawah Island, S.C.; Milo Stewart Jr., National Baseball Hall of Fame; Cooperstown, N.Y.; George Theofiles, "Miscellaneous Man," New Freedom, Pa.

PICTURE CREDITS

The sources for the illustrations in this book appear below. Credits from left to right are separated by semicolons; credits from top to bottom are separated by dashes.

Cover and dust jacket: U.S. Army Photo, courtesy of the Patton Museum, Fort Knox, Ky.; UPI/Corbis-Bettmann; Archive Photos, New York; Philippe Halsman, © Halsman Estate; National Archives from Corbis Digital Stock; AP/Wide World Photos; Frank Driggs Collection—National Archives Neg. No. 999-W & C-1221.

3: National Archives. **6, 7:** Courtesy John Robert Slaughter; Robert Capa/Magnum Photos, Inc., New York. **8, 9:** National Archives from Corbis Digital Stock. **10, 11:** National Archives from Corbis Digital Stock. **12, 13:** George Silk, *Life* Magazine © Time Inc. **14, 15:** G. Petrusov/Sovfoto, New York. **16, 17:** Marie Hansen, *Life* Magazine © Time Inc. **19:** Imperial War Museum, London, Neg. No. BH1306. **20:** Roger-Viollet, Paris. **22, 23:** CEKAP, Rome. **24, 25:** AP/Wide World Photos. **26:** Sovfoto, New York. **28, 29:** AP/Wide World Photos. **30, 31:** Josef Mucha/Czech News Agency, Prague. **32:** Hershenson-Allen Archive, West Plains, Mo.—Culver Pictures Inc., New York. **33:** Courtesy Stan Cohen, Missoula, Mont.—AP/Wide World Photos. **34, 35:** Hake's Americana & Collectibles, York, Pa. (3); John D. Collins; copyright © 1940 by *The New York Times*. Reprinted by permission. **36:** National Archives from Corbis Digital Stock. **37:** UPI/Corbis-Bettmann. **38, 39:** National Archives from Corbis Digital Stock. **40:** U.S. Navy W-PH-67-13982. **41:** AP/Wide World Photos. **42, 43:** Courtesy Antonio Alcalá; UPI/Corbis-Bettmann. **44, 45:** AP/Wide World Photos. **46:** Library of Congress, photographed by Henry Beville—George Strock, *Life* Magazine © Time Inc. **47:** National Archives, Neg. No. 80-G-472375. **48:** Alfred Eisenstaedt © Time Inc. Photo courtesy Kate Sheenan Hartson. **49:** *Los Angeles Times* Photo—Alfred Eisenstaedt, *Life* Magazine © Time Inc. **50:** UPI/Corbis-Bettmann; courtesy Gary Skoloff (2)—courtesy Hake's Americana & Collectibles, York, Pa.; courtesy Gary Skoloff—courtesy Hake's Americana & Collectibles, York, Pa. (2). **51:** Courtesy Gary Skoloff; courtesy Stan Cohen, Missoula, Mont. (3)—courtesy Gary Skoloff (3). **52:** W. Eugene Smith/Black Star, New York. **53:** Hershenson-Allen Archive, West Plains, Mo.; Movie Still Archives, Harrison, Nebr.—Al Freni/*Life* Magazine—Penguin/Corbis-Bettmann. **54, 55:** National Archives Neg. No. 208-AA-288BB-2; Mel Jacoby/*Life* Magazine. **56:** National Archives Neg. No. 1142-208AA-80B-1—National Archives Neg. No. 210-CC-S-26C. **57:** Photograph by Toyo Miyatake, copyright by Archie Miyatake, all rights reserved. **58, 59:** Gordon Coster, *Life* Magazine © Time Inc.; Hershenson-Allen Archive, West Plains, Mo. (2); Peter Stackpole, *Life* Magazine © Time Inc.—Franklin D. Roosevelt Library, Neg. No. NPx 51-115:169. **60:** U.S. Air Force Photo. **61:** AP/Wide World Photos; from the Doolittle collection of Ted Briscoe, San Jose, Calif. **62, 63:** The Boeing Company Archives, Seattle, Wash.; Detroit Historical Museum—© 1998 Journal Sentinel Inc., Milwaukee, Wis., reproduced with permission. **64, 65:** National Archives; Margaret Bourke-White, *Life* Magazine © Time Inc.—printed by permission of the Norman Rockwell Family Trust Copyright © 1943 the Norman Rockwell Family Trust; UPI/Corbis-Bettmann. **66, 67:** U.S. Navy Neg. No. 080-G-414423. **68, 69:** National Archives, Neg. No. 127-N-74085. **70, 71:** National Archives from Corbis Digital Stock. **72, 73:** National Archives Neg. No. 208-PU-138LL-3; UPI/Corbis-Bettmann;

Imperial War Museum, London. **74:** Courtesy Glen Ruh (3)—National Archives from *V Is for Victory* by Kathleen Krull, Apple Soup Books, Alfred A. Knopf, Inc., New York 1995—courtesy Harris Andrews (3). **75:** Kenneth Fleck, courtesy *Toys Go to War* by Jack Matthews, Pictorial Histories Publishing Company, Inc., Missoula, Mont. 1994; Kari Haavisto, New York—courtesy Jack Matthews (2)—courtesy Harris Andrews; courtesy Jack Matthews. **76:** Movie Still Archives, Harrison, Nebr. **77:** Movie Still Archives, Harrison, Nebr.; © 1944 George Baker—private collection—Edward Hopper, American, 1882-1967, *Nighthawks*, oil on canvas, 1942, Friends of American Art Collection, 1942.51 photograph © 1998, The Art Institute of Chicago. All Rights Reserved. **78, 79:** National Archives, Neg. No. 080-G-35190; UPI/Corbis-Bettmann. **80:** Map by John Drummond © Time Life Inc.—Library of Congress, from *The Largest Event* by Peter T. Rohrbach, Library of Congress, Washington, 1994. **81:** Photo by Al Freni, New York—Hart Preston, *Life* Magazine © Time Inc. **82:** Robert Capa/Magnum Photos, Inc., New York. **83:** UPI/Corbis-Bettmann. **84:** AP/Wide World Photos. **85:** Kari Haavisto, New York; courtesy Stan Cohen, Missoula, Mont.—courtesy Trudy Walker Pearson—Library of Congress. **86:** National Archives; UPI/Corbis-Bettmann—printed by permission of the Norman Rockwell Family Trust, copyright © 1943 the Norman Rockwell Family Trust. Photo courtesy U.S. Infantry Museum, Fort Benning, Ga. **87:** UPI/Corbis-Bettmann. **88:** U.S. Air Force Photo Neg. No. 26052—Margaret Bourke-White, *Life* Magazine © Time Inc. **89:** Imperial War Museum, London. **90:** U.S. Air Force. **91:** National Archives; Library of Congress, photographs by Al Freni (2). **92:** George Karger © Time Inc. **93:** UPI/Corbis-Bettmann; courtesy USO World Headquarters, Washington, D.C.—George Silk, *Life* Magazine © Time Inc.—Ralph Crane, *Life* Magazine © Time Inc. **94:** National Archives—National Archives Neg. No. 111-SC-203412. **95:** Lou Valentino Collection (3); R. R. Stuart Collection; Frank Driggs Collection. **96:** Map by John Drummond © Time Life Inc. **97:** U.S. Marine Corps Photo. **98:** W. Eugene Smith, *Life* Magazine © Time Inc. **99:** National Archives Neg. No. 127-GR-137-69889-13. **100, 101:** Courtesy Estate of Henry and Bella Kagan. **102:** Herbert Gehr, *Life* Magazine © Time Inc. **103:** Gjon Mili, *Life* Magazine © Time Inc.; Hershenson-Allen Archive, West Plains, Mo.—courtesy Jed Collectibles, Pemberton, N.J. **104, 105:** U.S. Army Air Force Photo. **106:** AP/Wide World Photos—National Archives Neg. No. 208-DA-6-2. **107:** John Phillips, *Life* Magazine © Time Inc.; reprinted by permission of Bill Mauldin and the Watkins/Loomis Agency. **108, 109:** National Archives Neg. No. 208-N-32987. **110, 111:** AP/Wide World Photos. **112, 113:** U.S. Coast Guard. **114, 115:** UPI/Corbis-Bettmann; U.S. Coast Guard Photo Neg. No. 2517. **116:** Corbis-Bettmann. **117:** National Archives Neg. No. 111-SC-191933. **118, 119:** Bob Landry, *Life* Magazine © Time Inc. **120:** U.S. Naval Historical Center Photograph, Neg. No. NH73070. **122:** National Archives Neg. No. 80-G-342482. **123:** National Archives Neg. No. 80-G-468912. **124:** ADN-ZB/Bundesarchiv, Koblenz. **125:** National Archives Neg. No. 111-SC-197304-S. **126:** U.S. Army Photo, SC-196304. **127:** Robert Capa/Magnum Photos, Inc., New York—Corbis-Bettmann. **128, 129:** Hershenson-Allen Archive, West Plains, Mo. except top left, courtesy Stan Cohen, Missoula, Mont. **130:** Movie Still Archives, Harrison, Nebr. **131:** National Baseball Hall of Fame Library, Cooperstown, N.Y.; National Baseball Hall of Fame Library, Cooperstown, N.Y., photo by Milo Stewart Jr.—Hershenson-Allen Archive, West Plains, Mo. **132:** Michael Ochs

Archives, Venice, Calif.; Glenn Miller Archive, University of Colorado at Boulder. **133:** Glenn Miller Archive, University of Colorado at Boulder. **134, 135:** Carl Mydans, *Life* Magazine © Time Inc.; National Archives Neg. No. 80-G-377613. **136, 137:** Sgt. Lou Lowery, *Leatherneck* Magazine. **138:** AP/Wide World Photos. **139:** Ullstein Bilderdienst, Berlin. **140:** George Silk, *Life* Magazine © Time Inc. **141:** National Archives Neg. No. 208-YE-132. **142, 143:** Margaret Bourke-White, *Life* Magazine © Time Inc. **144:** AP/Wide World Photos—A. Y. Owen (3). **145:** Copyright © 1945 by *The New York Times.* Reprinted by permission; Thomas D. McAvoy, *Life* Magazine © Time Inc. **146, 147:** AP/Wide World Photos. **148, 149:** National Archives from Corbis Digital Stock. **150, 151:** W. Eugene Smith, *Life* Magazine © Time Inc.; photo taken by *European Stars and Stripes* photographer Bud Kane. **152, 153:** UPI/Corbis-Bettmann—Los Alamos National Laboratory. **154:** O.W.I.-National Archives. **155:** Photo by Yosuke Yamahata © Shogo Yamahata. **156, 157:** U.S. Army Neg. No. SC-210241; Alfred Eisenstaedt, *Life* Magazine © Time Inc. **158, 159:** Carl Mydans, *Life* Magazine © Time Inc. **160:** Jack Manning-Pix Inc. **161:** Copyright Miss America Organization, Atlantic City, N.J.; private collection—Hershenson-Allen Archive, West Plains, Mo.—Jerry Cooke/*Life* Magazine.

162, 163: George Lyons, courtesy *The Boston Globe*; AP/Wide World Photos. **164, 165:** UPI/Corbis-Bettmann; Leonard McCombe, *Life* Magazine © Time Inc. **166:** George Skadding, *Life* Magazine © Time Inc.—Bob Campbell/U.S. Marine Corps Photo. **167:** Ed Clark, *Life* Magazine © Time Inc. **168:** UPI/Corbis-Bettmann—Cornell Capa, *Life* Magazine © Time Inc. **169:** UPI/Corbis-Bettmann. **170, 171:** no credit. **172:** © American Stock/Camerique, Blue Bell, Pa; Nina Leen, *Life* Magazine © Time Inc.; Tim Street-Porter, Hollywood, Calif.—Philippe Halsman © Halsman Estate—Nina Leen-Pix (2)—Philippe Halsman © Halsman Estate. **173:** Nina Leen, *Life* Magazine © Time Inc.; Irving Penn courtesy *Vogue*. **174, 175:** UPI/Corbis-Bettmann. **176:** Hy Peskin, *Life* Magazine © Time Inc. **177:** National Baseball Hall of Fame Library, Cooperstown, N.Y.—George Silk, *Life* Magazine © Time Inc. **178:** George Lacks, *Life* Magazine © Time Inc.; Waller/American Red Cross, Falls Church, Va. **179:** Walter Sanders, *Life* Magazine © Time Inc. **180, 181:** W. Eugene Smith, *Life* Magazine © Time Inc. **182:** Jack Koffman. **183:** Hershenson-Allen Archive, West Plains, Mo.; Eliot Elisofon, *Life* Magazine © Time Inc.—Corbis-Bettmann; *Daily Mirror*/Corbis-Bettmann. **184:** Bob Landry, *Life* Magazine © Time Inc. **185:** Philippe Halsman © Halsman Estate.

BIBLIOGRAPHY

BOOKS

Aaseng, Nathan. *Navajo Code Talkers.* New York: Walker, 1992.

Adams, Henry, and the Editors of Time-Life Books. *Italy at War* (World War II series). Alexandria, Va.: Time-Life Books, 1982.

African-American Sports Greats: A Biographical Dictionary. Ed. by David L. Porter. Westport, Conn.: Greenwood Press, 1995.

The Aftermath: Asia (World War II series). Alexandria, Va.: Time-Life Books, 1983.

Ambrose, Stephen E.:

Americans at War. Jackson: University Press of Mississippi, 1997.

Citizen Soldiers. New York: Simon & Schuster, 1997.

America in the '40s: A Sentimental Journey. Pleasantville, N.Y.: Reader's Digest, 1998.

American Decades: 1940-1949. Ed. by Victor Bondi. Detroit: Gale Research, 1995.

Bailey, Ronald H., and the Editors of Time-Life Books:

The Air War in Europe (World War II series). Alexandria, Va.: Time-Life Books, 1981.

The Home Front: U.S.A. (World War II series). Alexandria, Va.: Time-Life Books, 1978.

Bartlett, John. *Familiar Quotations* (16th ed.). Boston: Little, Brown, 1992.

The Baseball Encyclopedia (10th ed.). New York: Macmillan, 1996.

Benét's Reader's Encyclopedia. Ed. by Bruce Murphy. New York: HarperCollins, 1996.

Bethell, Nicholas, and the Editors of Time-Life Books. *Russia Besieged* (World War II series). Alexandria, Va.: Time-Life Books, 1977.

Blumenson, Martin, and the Editors of Time-Life Books. *Liberation* (World War II series). Alexandria, Va.: Time-Life Books, 1978.

Botting, Douglas, and the Editors of Time-Life Books. *The D-Day Invasion* (World War II series). Alexandria, Va.: Time-Life Books, 1978.

Bridgman, Jon. *The End of the Holocaust: The Liberation of the Camps.* Portland, Oreg.: Areopagitica Press, 1990.

Brimner, Larry Dane. *Voices From the Camps: Internment of Japanese Americans During World War II.* New York: Franklin Watts, 1994.

Buckley, Gail Lumet. *The Hornes: An American Family.* New York: Alfred A. Knopf, 1986.

Burns, James MacGregor. *Roosevelt: The Soldier of Freedom.* New York: Harcourt Brace Jovanovich, 1970.

Coffey, Frank. *Always Home: 50 Years of the USO—The Official Photographic History.* New York: Brassey's (US), 1991.

Cohen, Stan. *V for Victory: America's Home Front During World War II.* Missoula, Mont.: Pictorial Histories Publishing, 1991.

Collier, Richard, and the Editors of Time-Life Books. *The War in the Desert* (World War II series). Alexandria, Va.: Time-Life Books, 1977.

Colman, Penny. *Rosie the Riveter: Women Working on the Home Front in World War II.* New York: Crown Publishers, 1995.

The Concise Columbia Encyclopedia (2nd ed.). New York: Columbia University Press, 1989.

Conroy, Robert. *The Battle of Bataan: America's Greatest Defeat.* London: Macmillan, 1969.

Dewey, Donald. *James Stewart: A Biography.* Atlanta: Turner Publishing, 1996.

Dick, Bernard F. *The Star-Spangled Screen: The American World War II Film.* Lexington: University Press of Kentucky, 1996.

Dupuy, Trevor Nevitt. *Chronological Military History of World War II.* New York: Franklin Watts, 1965.

Eisenhower, Dwight D. *Crusade in Europe.* Garden City, N.Y.: Doubleday, 1948.

Encyclopedia of World Biography (2nd ed.) (Vols. 5, 7, 14). Detroit: Gale Research, 1998.

Erenberg, Lewis A. *Swingin' the Dream: Big Band Jazz and the Rebirth of American Culture.* Chicago: University of Chicago Press, 1998.

Fishgall, Gary. *Pieces of Time: The Life of James Stewart.* New York: Scribner, 1997.

Francis, Charles E. *The Tuskegee Airmen: The Men Who Changed a Nation.* Boston: Branden Publishing, 1993.

Frank, Richard B. *Guadalcanal.* New York: Random House, 1990.

Fremon, David K. *Japanese-American Internment in American History.* Springfield, N.J.: Enslow Publishers, 1996.

Gailey, Harry A. *The War in the Pacific: From Pearl Harbor to Tokyo Bay.* Novato, Calif.: Presidio, 1995.

Goodwin, Doris Kearns. *No Ordinary Time: Franklin and Eleanor Roosevelt, The Home Front in World War II.* New York: Simon & Schuster, 1994.

Goolrick, William K., Ogden Tanner, and the Editors of Time-Life Books. *The Battle of the Bulge* (World War II series). Alexandria, Va.: Time-Life Books, 1979.

Gordon, Lois G., and Alan Gordon. *American Chronicle: Six Decades in American Life, 1920-1980.* New York: Atheneum, 1987.

Greenberg, Milton. *The GI Bill: The Law That Changed America.* New York: Lickle Publishing, 1997.

Griffith, Richard, and Arthur Mayer. *The Movies.* New York: Simon &

Schuster, 1970.

Hackett, David A. (ed. and trans.). *The Buchenwald Report.* Boulder, Colo.: Westview Press, 1995.

Hassan, John (ed.). *The 1997 Information Please® Sports Almanac.* Boston: Houghton Mifflin, 1996.

Herzstein, Robert Edwin, and the Editors of Time-Life Books. *The Nazis* (World War II series). Alexandria, Va.: Time-Life Books, 1980.

Hickok, Ralph. *A Who's Who of Sports Champions.* Boston: Houghton Mifflin, 1995.

Higham, Charles, and Joel Greenberg. *Hollywood in the Forties.* London: A. Zwemmer, 1968.

Hirschhorn, Clive. *The Hollywood Musical.* New York: Crown Publishers, 1981.

Hoopes, Roy. *When the Stars Went to War: Hollywood and World War II.* New York: Random House, 1994.

Jablonski, Edward, and the Editors of Time-Life Books. *America in the Air War* (The Epic of Flight series). Alexandria, Va.: Time-Life Books, 1982.

Japan at War (World War II series). Alexandria, Va.: Time-Life Books, 1980.

Johnson, Susan E. *When Women Played Hardball.* Seattle: Seal Press, 1994.

Jones, Landon Y. *Great Expectations: America and the Baby Boom Generation.* New York: Coward, McCann & Geoghegan, 1980.

Kaplan, Philip, and Jack Currie. *Round the Clock: The Experience of the Allied Bomber Crews Who Flew by Day and by Night From England in the Second World War.* New York: Random House, 1993.

Katz, Ephraim. *The Film Encyclopedia.* New York: Thomas Y. Crowell, 1979.

Kavanagh, Jack, and James Tackach. *Great Athletes of the 20th Century.* New York: Gallery Books, 1989.

Koerner, Julie. *Swing Kings.* New York: Friedman/Fairfax, 1997.

Koppes, Clayton R., and Gregory D. Black. *Hollywood Goes to War.* Berkeley: University of California Press, 1987.

Krull, Kathleen. *V Is for Victory: America Remembers World War II.* New York: Alfred A. Knopf, 1995.

Lend Me Your Ears: Great Speeches in History. New York: W. W. Norton, 1992.

Life Goes to War: A Picture History of World War II. Boston: Little, Brown, 1977.

Life's Picture History of World War II. New York: Time, 1950.

Longford, Elizabeth. *Winston Churchill.* Chicago: Rand McNally, 1974.

McClain, S. *Navajo Weapon.* Boulder, Colo.: Books Beyond Borders, 1994.

Macdonald, John. *Great Battles of World War II.* New York: Macmillan, 1986.

McIntosh, Elizabeth P. *Sisterhood of Spies: The Women of the OSS.* Annapolis, Md.: Naval Institute Press, 1998.

Manchester, William. *The Last Lion, Winston Spencer Churchill: Visions of Glory, 1874-1932.* Boston: Little, Brown, 1983.

Marx, Arthur. *The Nine Lives of Mickey Rooney.* Briarcliff Manor, N.Y.: Stein and Day, 1986.

Mason, John T., Jr. (ed.). *The Pacific War Remembered.* Annapolis, Md.: Naval Institute Press, 1986.

Messenger, Charles. *The Pictorial History of World War II.* New York: Gallery Books, 1987.

Moody, Sidney C., Jr. *War Against Japan.* Novato, Calif.: Presidio, 1994.

1943: Turning the Tide. [Washington, D.C.]: United States Postal Service, 1993.

Our Glorious Century. Pleasantville, N.Y.: Reader's Digest, 1994.

The Oxford Companion to World War II. Oxford: Oxford University Press, 1995.

The Oxford Dictionary of Quotations (3rd ed.). Oxford: Oxford University Press, 1980.

The Oxford Dictionary of Quotations (rev. 4th ed.). Ed. by Angela Partington. Oxford: Oxford University Press, 1996.

The Oxford History of World Cinema. Ed. by Geoffrey Nowell-Smith. Oxford: Oxford University Press, 1996.

Perseverance (African Americans: Voices of Triumph series). Alexandria, Va.: Time-Life Books, 1993.

Pitts, Michael R. *Kate Smith.* New York: Greenwood Press, 1988.

Reach for Empire (The Third Reich series). Alexandria, Va.: Time-Life Books, 1989.

Reporting World War II (Part Two: American Journalism 1944-1946). New York: Library of America, 1995.

Rhodes, Richard. *The Making of the Atomic Bomb.* New York: Simon & Schuster, 1986.

Rice, William T. *The Pearl Harbor Story.* Hawaii: Hagadone Printing, 1996.

Rohrbach, Peter T. *The Largest Event.* Washington, D.C.: Library of Congress, 1994.

Rooney, Mickey. *Life Is Too Short.* New York: Villard Books, 1991.

Scott, John Anthony. *The Story of America.* Washington, D.C.: National Geographic Society, 1992.

The Second World War: Europe and the Mediterranean. Wayne, N.J.: Avery Publishing, 1984.

Shadow of the Dictators: TimeFrame AD 1925-1950 (Time Frame series). Alexandria, Va.: Time-Life Books, 1989.

Shaw, John, and the Editors of Time-Life Books. *Red Army Resurgent* (World War II series). Alexandria, Va.: Time-Life Books, 1979.

Sinnott, Susan. *Our Burden of Shame.* New York: Franklin Watts, 1995.

Slackman, Michael. *Remembering Pearl Harbor: The Story of the USS Arizona Memorial.* Honolulu: Arizona Memorial Museum, 1984.

Soames, Mary. *Family Album: A Personal Selection From Four Generations of Churchills.* Boston: Houghton Mifflin, 1982.

Stein, R. Conrad. *Battle of Guadalcanal.* Chicago: Childrens Press, 1983.

Steinberg, Rafael, and the Editors of Time-Life Books:
Island Fighting (World War II series). Alexandria, Va.: Time-Life Books, 1978.
Return to the Philippines (World War II series). Alexandria, Va.: Time-Life Books, 1979.

Sulzberger, C. L., and the Editors of *American Heritage. The American Heritage Picture History of World War II.* New York: American Heritage, 1994.

Szasz, Ferenc Morton. *The Day the Sun Rose Twice.* Albuquerque: University of New Mexico Press, 1984.

Thomas, Tony. *The Films of the Forties.* Secaucus, N.J.: Citadel Press, 1975.

Time Capsule (5 vols., 1941-1945). New York: Time-Life Books, 1967-1968.

To Win the War: Home Front Memorabilia of World War II. Missoula, Mont., 1995.

200 Years: A Bicentennial Illustrated History of the United States. Washington, D.C.: Books by U.S. News & World Report, 1973.

U.S. Camera 1944. New York: Duell, Sloan & Pearce, 1943.

Verges, Marianne. *On Silver Wings.* New York: Ballantine Books, 1991.

Wallace, Robert, and the Editors of Time-Life Books. *The Italian Campaign* (World War II series). Alexandria, Va.: Time-Life Books, 1978.

War and Conflict. Ed. by Jonathan Heller. Washington, D.C.: National Archives and Records Administration, 1990.

Ward, Geoffrey C. *Baseball: An Illustrated History.* New York: Alfred A. Knopf, 1994.

Wernick, Robert, and the Editors of Time-Life Books. *Blitzkrieg* (World War II series). Alexandria, Va.: Time-Life Books, 1976.

Wheeler, Keith, and the Editors of Time-Life Books. *The Road to Tokyo* (World War II series). Alexandria, Va.: Time-Life Books, 1979.

Williams, Vera S. *WACs: Women's Army Corps.* Osceola, Wis.: Motorbooks, 1997.

The World at Arms: The Reader's Digest Illustrated History of World War II. London: Reader's Digest, 1989.

World War II (The American Story series). Alexandria, Va.: Time-Life Books, 1997.

World War II: Personal Accounts, Pearl Harbor to V-J Day. Austin, Tex.: Lyndon Baines Johnson Foundation, 1992.

Zich, Arthur, and the Editors of Time-Life Books. *The Rising Sun* (World War II series). Alexandria, Va.: Time-Life Books, 1977.

PERIODICALS
"D-Day, Eyewitness to the Invasion." *Newsweek*, May 23, 1994.
Laurence, William L. "The Atomic Bomb." *New York Times*, n.d.
Murphy, Charles J. V. "China Reborn." *Life*, November 5, 1945.
Nelan, Bruce W. "Ike's Invasion." *Time*, June 6, 1994.
"1945." *Life: Special Collector's Edition*, June 5, 1995.
"Pearl Harbor: December 7, 1941-December 7, 1991." *Life: Collector's Edition*, Fall 1991.

Walsh, Michael. "The Longest Reign." *Time*, January 16, 1989.
"With Grief, We Bid You Farewell." *Time*, March 6, 1989.
"World War II." *Life: Special Issue*, Spring-Summer 1985.

OTHER SOURCES
"A Brief History of the AAGPBL." Available: http://baseballhalloffame.org/ exhibits/women/history.html November 3, 1998.
"Dorothy Kamenshek: First (Rockford Peaches)." Available: http://www.majorleaguebaseball.com/women/kamenshek.html November 3, 1998.

INDEX

TIME® LIFE BOOKS

Time-Life Books is a division of Time Life Inc.

TIME LIFE INC.
PRESIDENT and CEO: George Artandi

TIME-LIFE BOOKS
PUBLISHER/MANAGING EDITOR: Neil Kagan
VICE PRESIDENT, MARKETING: Joseph A. Kuna

OUR AMERICAN CENTURY

EDITORS: Loretta Britten, Paul Mathless
DIRECTOR, NEW PRODUCT DEVELOPMENT:
Elizabeth D. Ward

Decade of Triumph: The 40s

Editor: Robert Somerville
Deputy Editor: Mary Mayberry
Design Director: Tina Taylor
Associate Editor/Research and Writing: Nancy Blodgett
Marketing Manager: Pamela Farrell
Assistant Product Manager: Terri Miller
Picture Associate: Anne Whittle
Senior Copyeditor: Anne Farr
Technical Art Specialist: John Drummond
Picture Coordinator: Betty H. Weatherley
Editorial Assistant: Christine Higgins

Design for **Our American Century** by Antonio Alcalá, Studio A, Alexandria, Virginia.

Special Contributors: Robert Speziale (editing); Ronald H. Bailey, Constance Buchanan, Janet Cave, Susan Perry (writing); Harris Andrews, Ruth Goldberg, Daniel Kulpinski, Jane Martin, Marilyn Terrell, Heidi Vogt (research and writing); Monika Lynde (production); Sunday Oliver (index).

Correspondents: Christine Hinze (London), Christina Lieberman (New York), Maria Vincenza Aloisi (Paris). Valuable assistance was also provided by Angelika Lemmer (Bonn).

Director of Finance: Christopher Hearing
Directors of Book Production: Marjann Caldwell, Patricia Pascale
Director of Publishing Technology: Betsi McGrath
Director of Photography and Research: John Conrad Weiser
Director of Editorial Administration: Barbara Levitt
Production Manager: Gertraude Schaefer
Quality Assurance Manager: James King
Chief Librarian: Louise D. Forstall

EDITORIAL CONSULTANT
Richard B. Stolley is currently senior editorial adviser at Time Inc. After 19 years at *Life* magazine as a reporter, bureau chief, and assistant managing editor, he became the first managing editor of *People* magazine, a position he held with great success for eight years. He then returned to *Life* magazine as managing editor and later served as editorial director for all Time Inc. magazines. In 1997 Stolley received the Henry Johnson Fisher Award for Lifetime Achievement, the magazine industry's highest honor.

Library of Congress Cataloging-in-Publication Data
Decade of triumph: the 40s / by the editors of Time-Life Books.
    p. cm.— (Our American century)
Includes bibliographical references and index.
ISBN 0-7835-5506-7
1. United States—History—1933-1945. 2. United States—
History—1945-1953.   3. Nineteen forties.
4. United States—History—1933-1945—Pictorial works.
5. United States—History—1945-1953—Pictorial works.
6. Nineteen forties—Pictorial works.
I. Time-Life Books.   II. Series.
E806.D425   1999
973.9—dc21   98-48383
                                               CIP

Other History Publications:

World War II
What Life Was Like
The American Story
Voices of the Civil War
The American Indians
Lost Civilizations
Mysteries of the Unknown
Time Frame
The Civil War
Cultural Atlas

For information on and a full description of any of the Time-Life Books series listed above, please call 1-800-621-7026 or write:

Reader Information
Time-Life Customer Service
P.O. Box C-32068
Richmond, Virginia 23261-2068